THE HISTORY OF

ANCIENT ASIA

THE HISTORY OF

ANCIENT ASIA

MEREDITH MACARDLE

WORTH
PRESS

First published in 2019 by Worth Press Ltd, Bath, England
worthpress@btconnect.com

British Library Cataloguing in Publication Data
A catalogue record for this book is available from the British Library

ISBN: 978-1-84931-162-5

10 9 8 7 6 5 4 3 2 1

Author's Acknowledgement
With thanks to Susan Boyd Lees, Declan MacArdle, Louise MacArdle, and Paul Russom for their help.

Publisher's Note Every effort has been made to ensure the accuracy of the information presented in this book. The publisher will not assume liability for damages caused by inaccuracies in the data and makes no warranty whatsoever expressed or implied. The publisher welcomes comments and corrections from readers, emailed to worthpress@btconnect.com, which will be considered for incorporation in future editions. Every effort has been made to trace copyright holders and seek permission to use illustrative and other material. The publisher wishes to apologize for any inadvertent errors or omissions and would be glad to rectify these in future editions.

The images used in this book come from either the public domain or from the public commons unless otherwise stated.

Design and layout: Chandra Creative & Content Solutions Pvt. Ltd.
Cover Design: Wayne Morrish

Printed and bound in China

HOW TO USE THE BOOK

Features section:
Provides information on various aspects of the evolution and history of the ancient civilizations of Asia.

Timeline section:
Entries on significant events flow down in chronological order (on blue background).

EAST ASIA: CHINA CHANGES

200 BCE–80 CE

After the decline of the Han dynasty in China, it would be several hundred years before the country enjoyed a matching period of dynamism and strength.

First, three kingdoms fought for supremacy, then the Western Jin dynasty that eventually emerged supreme was overrun by nomads from the north and abandoned control over the Yellow River valley. Under the Eastern Jin, the capital moved to what is now Nanjing. The country split again into Northern and Southern Dynasties, before finally the Sui took a grip on the seat of power in 581.

The Sui made a good start. They opened examination centers for the civil service all round the country, instead of just at the capital, allowing more candidates to apply to be government officials. This had the effect of raising standards overall. The Sui

A Sui-Dynasty Buddhist bodhisattva statue.

A Sui-Dynasty "wu zhu" coin. Named after their weight (one zhu weighed 100 millet seeds and the coin weighed five zhus), wu zhus were minted for hundreds of years.

also reformed the legal code, and built the Great Canal, linking the Yellow and the Yangtze rivers. They then made a costly mistake, launching other expensive and ambitious projects that needed conscripted labor. By 605 the spirit of rebellion was in the air again.

China ended this early period of its history with another major change underway. For a long time no one had been able to offer strong leadership and defend the borders, and as a result northern China had been suffering from the curse of bandit raids. By 400 CE people were drifting away from this danger zone to the lower Yangtze valley, even though it was full of swamps and jungles that had to be cleared and drained through canals, reservoirs, and dams. Slowly, the Yangtze valley's agricultural output began to outstrip that of the North China Plain.

200 China attempts to crush the Mongolian Xiongnu but is defeated. The two states divide their territory at the Great Wall.
164 According to tradition, Prince Liu An from northern China creates tofu, or bean curd, by pressing coagulated soy milk into chunks.
150 The Xiongnu cross the Great Wall and take control of China north of the Yellow River.
138 Chinese General Zhang Qian is sent into the West to find allies against the Xiongnu. His reports on people and routes are said to be the beginning of the Silk Roads, the overland trade routes from China to the West.
128 An overland trade route between China and India is forged across northern Burma.
121 China repels the Xiongnu and pushes them north of the Gobi desert.
111 China conquers a large part of Vietnam.
108 China founds colonies in Manchuria and northern Korea.
100 In the Bronze Age the Malay Peninsula becomes a maritime trading crossroads for goods from India, Egypt, the Middle East, Java and China.
91 Sima Qian, the "father of Chinese historians," completes his literary history of China.
c.60 Having been displaced by the Mongolian Xiongnu, a group of nomadic Yuezhi people begin to form the Kushan Empire centered in Afghanistan. The Kushans will help develop the Silk Roads and allow Buddhism to be transmitted to China.
9–23 CE The Xin (New) dynasty in China rebels against the Han and ends abuses by landowners and nobles.
25 CE The New Eastern Han dynasty overthrows the Xin in China.
57 A Chinese record is the first written mention of Japan.
68 Buddhist monks from India arrive in China.
80 Burial of the "Jade Princess," Princess Douwan, in China. Her burial suit is made of 2,160 pieces of jade sewn together by gold wire.

242

243

Front cover: 17th-century map of Asia.
Inside front cover and front cover flap: Sunset over the ruins of Ephesus, Turkey.
Back cover (inset): The Gypsy Girl Mosaic, Gaziantep, Turkey.
Inside back cover and back cover flap: Ming dynasty guardian lion in the Forbidden City, Beijing.

CONTENTS

Ancient Asia first saw human societies take some giant steps forward. The great river valleys of the continent were home to people who independently discovered the advantages of agriculture, invented writing, built cities, and developed into great civilizations. These ancient Asian civilizations left a magnificent heritage, giving us the Law Code of Hammurabi, the Terracotta Army, and ritual bathing, among other tangible and intangible legacies.

The continent was also home to some of the world's major religions, including Hinduism, Buddhism, and the three monotheistic faiths of Judaism, Christianity, and Islam.

Of course, there was nothing specifically "Asian" about these societies; none of these ancient people would have thought of themselves as "Asian." The idea of separate continents was a much later human concept. The ancient Greeks first used the word "Asia" for the lands to their east – Asia Minor and Persia – just as they labeled everyone to their south along the Mediterranean as "Libyans," and "Europeans" were from the lands to the west of the Greek world. All these names derived from demi-goddesses. Later, the term "Asia" was applied to other countries in the east.

Technically, of course, Eurasia is one landmass, and is even connected to Africa

China's Terracotta Army in Xi'an.

by the narrow strip of land that is now bisected by the Suez Canal. So, in that respect, modern continental divisions could be described as somewhat arbitrary. By around 1850, mapmakers were placing Asia east of the Ural Mountains and south of the Caucasus Mountains and the Black Sea. The Sinai Peninsula and Cyprus were included in Asia. Oceans form the continent's other boundaries: the Arctic, the Indian, and the Pacific. Some Indonesian islands are not part of Asia.

This means that Kazakhstan, Russia, and Turkey all have parts of their countries in Europe, as well as in Asia. In Turkey's case the Asian part, the Anatolian peninsula, is also known as Asia Minor. While the modern city of Istanbul in Turkey is the world's only city to straddle two contents, its ancient parts of Byzantium and Constantinople were in Europe.

There is no one agreed-on date for the end of the ancient world. The transition to the modern world or to a middle age happened in different areas at different times. In West Asia, the Muslim Arabs brought an end to ancient societies, so this book takes 610 CE as its end date, the year that Muhammad first received the revelations that would lead to the religion of Islam.

Moses and the Ten Commandments by Henry Schile, 1874.

Steps of the Ziggurat of Ur built by the Neo-Sumerians.

A 17th-century map of Asia.

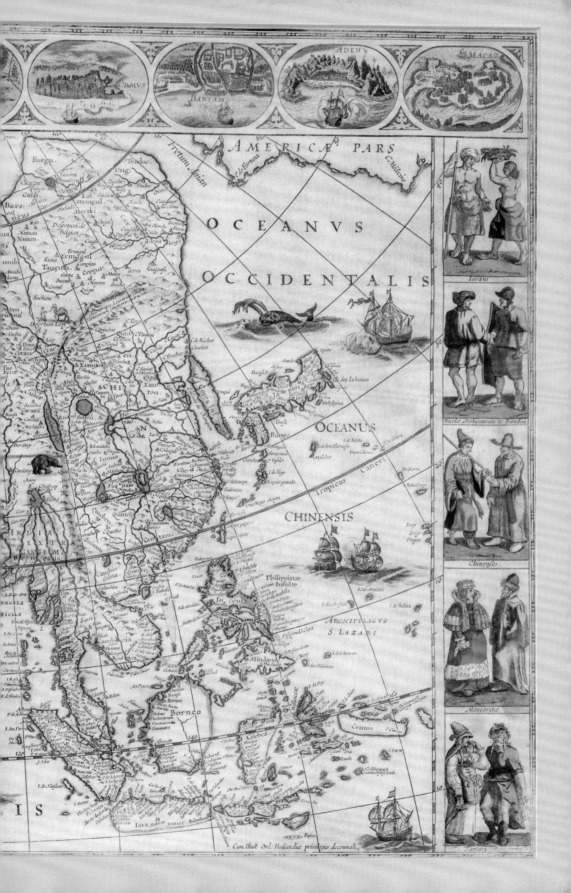

ANCIENT ASIA'S CIVILIZATIONS

HISTORY OF ASIA - MAJOR CIVILIZATIONS

NB: Many dates are approximate

BCE

		4000	3750	3500	3250	3000	2750	2500

West Asia

Mesopotamia	Sumeria (3500–2300)
	Akkadia (2300–1894)
	Babylonia (1894–539)
	Middle Assyrian Empire (1340–1032)
	Neo-Assyria (911–609)
Iran	Kingdom of Elam (2000–640)
	Achaemenid/Persian Empire (550–334)
	Alexander the Great Empire (334–321)
	Seleucid Empire (312–63)
	Parthian Empire (171–224 CE)
	Sasanian Empire (224–651)
Palestine/Israel/ Levant	Phoenicia (1550–300)
	Sea Peoples (1276–1178)
	Israelites (1200–1000)
	Kingdom of David and Solomon (1000–924)
	Kingdoms of Israel and Judah (924–142)
	Hasmonean Dynasty, Judah (142–63)
	Palmyrene Empire (267–270)
Arabia	Dilmun (c. 3000–c. 540)
	Nabataeans (85–106 CE)
Turkey	Hittites (2000–1193)
	Troy (1500–1000)
South Asia-India	Indus Valley (height) (2400–1800)
	Vedic Period (1500–500)
	Mauryan Empire (321–185)
	Guptas (320–6th century CE)
East Asia-China	Shang Dynasty (1600–1046)
	Zhou Dynasty (1046–770)
	Warring Sates (770–221)
	Qin Emperors (221–206)
	Han Dynasty (206–220 CE)
Central Asia	Scythia (c. 900 BCE–400 CE)
	Xiongnu Confederacy (209 BCE–93 CE)

A silver drachma coin of Arsaces I, the founder of the Arsacid Dynasty, includes an inscription of his name in Greek.

The Warka Vase is a carved alabaster stone vessel found in the temple complex of the Sumerian goddess Inanna in the ruins of the ancient city of Uruk, southern Iraq.

A Hittite legal tablet, written in cuneiform, with an "envelope" and witness seals.

Seals from Mohenjo-daro.

Bronze cooking vessel, Shang Dynasty.

This figured vessel shows the skill of Scythian artists.

Nimrud.

The headless
statue of Queen
Napirasu.

The Hanging Gardens of
Babylon.

A bronze spearhead from
China's Eastern Zhou dynasty,
5th century BCE.

The world's largest continent, Asia naturally has a huge range of terrains, geographical regions, and wildlife. It is home to the highest and lowest points on earth: measured from sea level, Mount Everest, straddling the border between Nepal and China in the Himalayas, is 29,029 feet (8,848 m) high, while the lowest point on dry land is the shore of the Dead Sea, shared by Israel, Jordan, and the Palestinian Territories, which is 1,419 feet (432.65 m) below sea level and dropping (since the Dead Sea

A sinkhole on the shores of the Dead Sea.

Mount Everest.

Rice terraces.

waters are receding, the surface level falls every year).

People have managed to live throughout Asia, even in the Arctic and Siberia in the north or the tropical jungles of the southeast. The fertile river valleys along the periphery of Asia saw the first civilizations, which were frequently raided by horse-riding nomads from the central plains. These nomads then found that the cramped agricultural areas – where land was so precious that tiny terraces were carved out of hillsides – did not have enough grasslands to support large herds. So back they went to the steppes, or adapted to a settled lifestyle.

The Himalayas and other mountain ranges block the warm and wet climate of the south, with its monsoons or tropical cyclones, from reaching Central Asia, which is predominantly dry steppes, as well as mountains or deserts.

THREATENED SPECIES

Asia's unique wildlife include many species that are now endangered because of habitat loss or over-hunting by humans. Threatened species include:

- *China's panda bear. There are fewer than 2,000 surviving in the wild.*
- *The Asian elephant from India and other tropical or subtropical areas of South and Southeast Asia.*
- *The single-horned Indian rhinoceros, now found only in India and Nepal.*
- *The Bengal tiger, with about 2,500 surviving in Bangladesh, Nepal, Bhutan, China, and Myanmar.*
- *The two-humped Bactrian camel of the deserts in southern Mongolia, northwestern China, and Kazakhstan.*
- *The Malayan tapir from the rainforests of Thailand, Myanmar, Malaysia, and Sumatra.*
- *The slow loris from the forests of southern Asia.*

Asia's biodiversity includes thousands more unique species, ranging from trees and shrubs to reptiles and fish, including such odd species as the hooded cobra, Japanese macaques or snow monkeys, and flying geckos.

The once endangered Arabian oryx has been reintroduced into the Arabian Desert, and although giant pandas are rare in China, their population is twice what it was in the 1970s. Some of Asia's vulnerable wild species are winning their fight to survive.

Arabian oryx.

Giant panda.

When members of the early human ancestor *Homo erectus* (upright man) left the evolutionary heartlands of Africa about 1.8 million years ago, they spread out throughout Europe and Asia

Although the fossil record is sketchy, remains of *Homo erectus* have been found in China dating to about 1.7 million years ago and in Java dating to about 1.5 million years ago. A later site in China, the Zhoukoudien cave near Beijing, was occupied intermittently

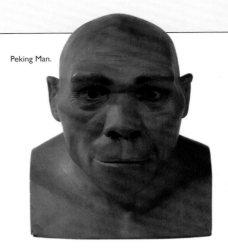

Peking Man.

NEANDERTHAL BURIALS

Evolving from *Homo erectus* sometime before 200,000 years ago, our close cousins the Neanderthals (*Homo neanderthalensis*) lived across a wide swathe of Eurasia from the Mediterranean to the Altai Mountains. Stockier than modern humans but large-brained and with a sophisticated tool kit, the Neanderthals were well-suited to survive in the Late Ice Age, but they died out some 30,000 years ago.

Asian sites offer some important data on Neanderthal life. At Shanidar in northern Iraq, several skeletons were found that showed signs of bad physical injuries that they nevertheless survived. One male would have been blind in one eye and only had the use of one arm, yet he was obviously cared for by the group. Most of the Shanidar skeletons were deliberately buried.

HOBBITS

Asia shows that there was a wide range of early human species. The Indonesian island of Flores was home to a group of tiny hominims called Homo floresiensis. Inevitably, they are popularly known as hobbits, although we do not know if they had hairy feet. The hobbits were about 3 feet 6 inches (1.1 m) tall, used stone tools, and hunted rodents and pygmy elephants that are now extinct. Their fossils date to between 100,000 and 60,000 years ago.

Model reconstruction of the head of a female *Homo floresiensis*.

by *Homo erectus* from about 770,000 years ago until relatively late, around 230,000 years ago. Known there as "Peking Man," it is possible some of these hominims practiced cannibalism.

The stone tools used by East Asian *Homo erectus* populations were different from those used elsewhere. Whereas in West Asia and Europe hand axes were a major part of the *erectus* tool kit, in China and Southeast Asia the emphasis was on pebble choppers and scrapers.

The interior view of the Shanidar cave.

Another deliberate burial was that of a Neanderthal boy in the cave of Teshik-Tash, southeastern Uzbekistan. Horns of a Siberian mountain goat were driven into the ground around the body.

Apart from these signs of ceremony, the jury is still out on whether the Neanderthals created art and had a symbolic life.

TIMELINE OF ASIA

1.8 million BCE *Homo erectus* migrates out of Africa to Southeast Asia, leaving stone handaxes in Lenggong, Malaysia.

1.5 million BCE *Homo erectus* migrates across the land bridges to Java (Java Man).

770,000 *Homo erectus* (Peking Man) is living in the Zhoukoudian caves in China.

100,000–60,000 Hobbits, the short hominim species *Homo floresiensis*, live on the Indonesian island of Flores.

90,000 The Denisova cave in the Altai Mountains of Siberia is home to a new species of archaic humans, *Homo denisova*. One of the bodies buried there is the daughter of a Neanderthal mother and a Denisovan father.

70,000 Modern human beings, *Homo sapiens sapiens*, have migrated from Africa throughout Asia.

60,000 Neanderthals in the Shanidar cave, northern Iraq, care for the injured and arrange a burial.

50,000 Modern human beings reach Australia from Southeast Asia.

40,000 The diet of early humans in Borneo includes orangutans.

40,000 Rock art in Southeast Asia is created in rock shelters, rather than in deep caves.

33,000 The earliest known domesticated dog is found in Siberia.

30,000–13,000 People migrate into America across the Bering Straits or by sea from Asia.

29,000 One of the last populations of Neanderthals survives in Russia.

20,000 The Japanese archipelago separates from the Asian continent.

18,000 The earliest known pottery vessels in the world are made in the Xianren Cave in Jingxi, China.

13,000 Cave paintings are made at Bhimbetka, India.

12,500 The world's earliest known bread, a flatbread from wild grains, is made at Shubayqa, Jordan.

11,000 The Natufian culture in the Levant is brewing beer from barley.

DENISOVANS – A NEW SPECIES

The Denisovans are thought to have evolved from the same branch of *Homo erectus* as the Neanderthals. Only identified as a separate archaic human species in 2010, their bones were found in the Denisova cave in Siberia's Altai Mountains, dating to around 90,000 years ago. Investigation of the bodies buried in the cave revealed one to be the daughter of a Neanderthal mother and a Denisovan father.

Denisovans also interbred with modern humans. Their DNA is found in small amounts in most Asians and also Native Americans, and in slightly higher proportions in Aboriginal Australians, Papuans, Melanesians, and some peoples in Southeast Asian islands. It is thought that Denisovan DNA might have helped Tibetan people adapt successfully to life at high altitude with low oxygen levels.

Russian archeologists digging inside the Denisova cave.

THE COMING OF THE HUMANS

It is thought that modern human beings – *Homo sapiens sapiens* – migrated out of Africa, where we evolved from another branch of *Homo erectus*, in two waves, around 100,000 years ago and around 70,000 years ago. So for a long period the earth was shared by at least three human species.

Scientists had speculated for a long time that modern humans and Neanderthals might have interbred, especially since some

skeletons seem to have features of both species. DNA evidence has now proven that nearly everyone today, including even some sub-Saharan African populations, has possibly 2 percent Neanderthal DNA. It is thought that part of our genetic inheritance from Neanderthals contributes to our immune systems.

Neanderthals probably died out for a combination of reasons: an inability to adapt to changing climatic conditions

c.11,000 BCE The Ain Sakhri lovers statuette, the earliest known depiction of a couple having sex, is left in the Ain Sakhri caves in the Judean Desert.

10,000 A wave of migration from southwest China takes people to Malaysia, then on to Indonesia, Sumatra, and Borneo, and probably on to Polynesia.

10,000 The Jomon culture develops in Japan with distinctive cord-marked pottery.

10,000 Pygmy hippopotamuses and dwarf elephants are probably hunted to extinction on Cyprus.

9500 The earliest known association of a human and a cat is in a burial site on Cyprus.

c.9130 The first megaliths are raised at Göbekli Tepe in Turkey.

9000–8000 West Asia sees the world's earliest developments in agriculture.

9000 The Natufian culture in West Asia makes the transition between hunter-gatherers and agriculturalists.

c.8800 Second phase of megaliths at Göbekli Tepe, Turkey.

c.8000 The town of Jericho is built in Palestine.

c.8000 Göbekli Tepe is abandoned.

7000 Barley and wheat are cultivated in Mesopotamia.

7000 Rice and millet are cultivated at Jiahu in China.

6800 The first signs of silkworm cultivation at Banpo, China.

c.6700 The village/town of Çatal Hüyük in Turkey is built.

6500 Early farming villages appear in the Indus Valley.

6500 Rice is part of the diet in India.

6000 Agriculture is now well-developed in Mesopotamia.

c.5650 Çatal Hüyük is abandoned.

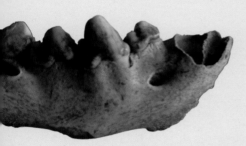

The remains of a prehistoric mammal bone which was found inside the Denisova cave.

as their usual prey, large game animals, became scarcer; failing to compete with modern human beings for resources; diseases carried by *Homo sapiens*, or just good, old-fashioned violence. They survived in Siberia longer than anywhere else in Eurasia, with the most recently known Neanderthal site at Byzovaya in Russia's subarctic Ural Mountains dating to 29,000 years ago.

THE DAY OF THE DOG

Probably the first animal to be domesticated by human beings was the dog, which was bred from wolf stock. The earliest skeleton of a domesticated dog was found in Siberia dating to 33,000 years ago, but it is thought that they were probably first domesticated in China, since that country has the greatest diversity of dog species.

When people left Asia and settled on the land bridge that used to exist between Siberia and Alaska before much later migrating onward to America, they took their dogs with them, since the earliest domesticated dogs found in America were all descendants of Chinese species.

THE FERTILE CRESCENT

A roughly semi-circular region running from the Nile Valley in Egypt, through the Palestinian Territories, Israel, Jordan, Syria, Lebanon, Cyprus, and Iraq, and including southern Turkey and southwestern Iran, the Fertile Crescent saw the earliest known examples of animal domestication and crop cultivation. Since animals need herding and crops need tending, people in the region began to settle down in permanent villages instead of continuing their ancestors' nomadic, hunter-gatherer lifestyle. Following the development of agriculture, this Fertile Crescent was also the home of some of the world's first complex societies, including Sumeria, the first civilization. For this reason the area is also sometimes called the "Cradle of Civilization."

Bounded by the Sahara Desert in the west, the Syrian Desert in the south, the Anatolian highlands in the north, and the Iranian Plateau in the east, when agriculture began to play a part in human lives around 9000–8000 BCE, the Fertile Crescent had a more moderate climate than today, so was probably better suited to farming. Most importantly, it contained large rivers: the Nile, Tigris, Euphrates, and Jordan. It was also home to the wild progenitors of early crops such as wheat, barley, peas, lentils, chickpeas, and flax, as well to cows, pigs, and goats, species which were first domesticated and farmed by humans.

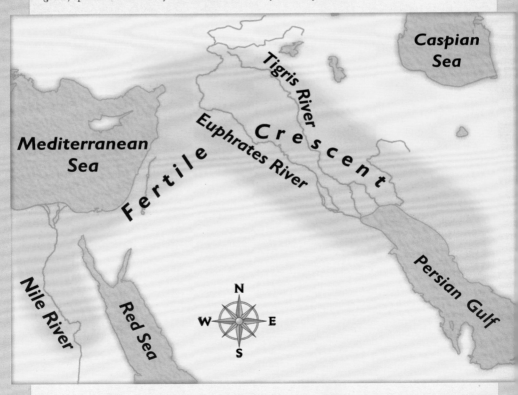

END OF THE STONE AGE

When modern human beings began to spread out through the world they were nomadic hunter-gatherers, using stone tools along with wood, antlers, ivory, shell, and bone. They made jewelry and small statues, and painted art on cave walls or rocks. By 40,000 years ago they had reached Borneo, and, as the most successful hominid species, were able to live in Russia's freezing north by 33,000 years ago.

This way of life continued for thousands of years before what has been called the "Neolithic Agricultural Revolution," when people of the New Stone Age began to settle down and farm their food instead of foraging for it, a process that began in Asia some time around 10,000 BCE.

5000 Rising waters submerge the land-bridge between India and Sri Lanka, creating the Java and South China Seas. Thousands of islands are left as part of Indonesia and the Philippines.

5000 In a new wave of human migration, indigenous people leave Taiwan and arrive in Polynesia.

5000 Indus Valley villages develop trade networks. Copper is used.

4700–4400 Domesticated peaches appear in Japan.

4000 The Longshan culture in China, distinguished by black pottery.

4000 Rice is cultivated in Thailand.

3500 The first evidence of domesticated horses, in present-day Kazakhstan. They may have been domesticated as early as 6000 on the Eurasian steppes.

Neolithic stone tools.

THE NATUFIANS: A PEOPLE IN TRANSITION

Centered in the Mediterranean Levant – Palestine, Israel, Syria, Lebanon, and Jordan – from about 13,000 to 9000 BCE, the Natufian culture, named after finds in the Wadi an-Natuf in the Judean Mountains, might have been the earliest to make the transition from Stone Age nomadic hunter-gatherers to settled farmers.

Although they were still mainly hunters, in the early phase of the culture the Natufians were semi-sedentary, living in caves or building semi-subterranean pit-houses. These had stone foundations, wooden walls and brush roofs. At this stage they did not deliberately plant crops, but simply gathered wild grain, but they made two important innovations: they developed sickle blades for intensive harvesting of cereals, and picks for cultivating the ground.

THE FIRST BEER

The Natufians innovated in another way: they also brewed the first known beer, out of barley. It is possible that beer was used in rituals, and some scientists suggest that because the Natufians needed a regular supply of barley for their ceremonies, they might have deliberately sown a crop rather than relying on finding enough wild stands of the cereal.

As with other late Stone Age people, Natufian stone tools were small blades set in bone or wooden hafts. The edges of their sickle blades are coated with a give-away gloss of silica remains that suggests cereal harvesting, a fact confirmed by microscopic cell analysis. Before the use of sickles, grain was gathered by beating it into baskets, a much less efficient process.

A pre-pottery culture, the Natufians had stone mortars and pestles for grinding their grain.

The change to crop cultivation was a process, not a single event, and the domestication of cereals could have occurred accidentally as a result of intensive harvesting. But by the late Natufian period, around 10,000 BCE, some of the wheat growing in the region had been domesticated to the forerunners of that grown today. One of the major changes was breeding a type of cereal where the seeds do not fall off the stalk when ripe, but remain in place so they can be easily harvested.

JERICHO'S WALLS

One of the earliest continuous towns in the world, Jericho in Palestine was seasonally occupied by Natufian hunter-gatherers from about 9000 BCE before it became a permanent settlement perhaps as early as 8000 BCE.

At around this time a strong stone wall, including a huge tower, was built around the town. Early houses were small and round, made of sun-dried clay and straw bricks with a mud plaster, and a noticeable feature was the burial of the dead under the house floors. Wheat and barley were cultivated.

Jericho's fortunes rose and fell over the next several thousand years, but it was continuously occupied, even if sometimes by small groups. Around 1900 BCE the varied peoples known as Canaanites lived there, and it was during their occupation that the Bible records Joshua leading the Israelites to destroy the town. Archeologists, can, however, find no trace of this event.

THE WORLD'S OLDEST TEMPLE

Once thought to be just a medieval cemetery, the mound of Göbekli Tepe (meaning Potbelly Hill) in southern Turkey concealed a unique archeological discovery. Believed to be the world's first temple, its massive stone blocks were built by hunter-gatherers before farming, before metal tools, and even before pottery.

About 980 feet (300 m) in diameter, the site dates back to the 10th millennium BCE, and may in fact be not one but several different centers of ritual and worship.

Phase one of Göbekli Tepe, from about 9130 BCE, involved the construction of the world's oldest known megaliths, or large, prehistoric stone monuments. Huge, T-shaped stone pillars were arranged in circular, walled compounds, each block up to 20 feet (6 m) tall and weighing up to 10 tons. More than 200 pillars in about 20 circles are at the site. Many stones have carvings of animals or abstract pictograms on their surfaces, all made by stone tools.

Some of the pillars have human arms or loincloths carved in their lower half, leading archeologists to speculate that they represent either people – perhaps ancestors – or gods. At the center of the circles there are two larger pillars facing each other.

Phase two, from around 8800 BCE, saw smaller pillars arranged in rectangular rooms, which had floors of polished lime. There is no evidence of settlement at the site, so archeologists believe it was a ritual center for people from a wide area nearby.

THE ARTS OF ÇATAL HÜYÜK

Dating to about 6700 BCE, the village/town of Çatal Hüyük in Turkey is an important example of a Neolithic settlement. Its inhabitants showed the transition from hunting and gathering to a fully settled lifestyle, relying on agriculture. Çatal Hüyük is extraordinary in two ways: first, there were no streets and no doors. The houses were built next to each other like cells in a beehive, and were entered through a hole in the flat roof, presumably by wooden ladders. There were large,

The early Neolithic "Seated Mother Goddess" statue, dating to about 6500 BCE, from Çatal Hüyük in Turkey.

communal ovens on the roofs, so probably the large area of adjacent roofs was used as a social space. Secondly, the town was covered by art.

With rectangular rooms built of mud-brick and plaster, the houses contained a hearth and a small oven, platforms for sitting, working, or sleeping, and almost all of them had highly decorated walls. Paintings or wall reliefs showed animals, people, and geometric patterns, and were frequently renewed, with the walls replastered then repainted.

Often, the houses also contained the

Then, some time around 8000 BCE, this massive religious site was no longer needed, and the compounds and rooms were carefully filled in.

Göbekli Tepe overturns the conventional theories of human progress, which hold that only after the "Neolithic Revolution," when people domesticated animals, grew crops, and thus settled down in farming communities, was there the social and religious organization that allowed huge monuments to be constructed. But Göbekli Tepe, built by Stone Age hunter-gatherers, showed as much sophistication as the first Neolithic buildings – and more artistic effort.

Göbekli sits at the northern edge of the Fertile Crescent, reinforcing just

The early Neolithic archeological site of Göbekli Tepe.

how important that region was to early humans. It still contains many mysteries — most of the site has not been excavated, and has been left for future archeologists who might have better tools to understand the past.

bodies of the dead, buried under floors or platforms. Bodies of children were covered with ochre and buried with beads, otherwise there was no distinction in burials between rich and poor.

However, separate religious areas were distinguished within the town. Some buildings were religious shrines, even more elaborately decorated in a style that is very similar to that of the cave paintings of Stone Age Europe, often showing animal heads. Like domestic buildings, the paintings were frequently renewed.

A huge number of sculptures in stone or clay, especially of women, were also found at Çatal Hüyük, leading many to speculate that there was a religion centered on a Mother Goddess. These figurines were found throughout the town, in walls, oven walls, and floors. Bone tools were also often finely decorated.

Another, extraordinary part of the inhabitants' interior design was the use of animal remains plastered into walls then painted. Bull skulls were the most commonly used ornaments, but horns, tusks, beaks, and skulls of other animals were also used.

Some archeologists think that this animal art is a recognition of the social change from hunting wild animals that had dangerous, pointed parts, to herding domesticated beasts. Certainly Çatal Hüyük's people grew cereal crops, cultivated seeds and nuts, and kept herds of cattle, as well as hunting other animals such as deer and wild boar. They made stone tools, wooden bowls, and pottery, wove baskets, and spun textiles. They also traded for shells, metals, and pigments that came from the Mediterranean or further afield.

Perhaps 8,000 people lived in Çatal Hüyük at its height, but some time around 5650 BCE this city of artists was abandoned.

TEN THOUSAND YEARS OF POTTERY

Agriculture did not begin in Japan until relatively late, during the Yayou Period beginning around 300 BCE, when rice farming was introduced. Up until then, it seems that the food resources were plentiful enough that the people of the previous Jomon Period had no need to cultivate crops, although the domesticated peach was introduced around 4700 BCE.

The Jomon people were an unusual mix of hunter-gatherers and proto-agriculturalists. They tended certain plants such as yams, nut trees, and soybeans, and lived a semi-sedentary lifestyle, but they mainly hunted, fished, and foraged for food.

Jomon means "cord marks," and the culture was named for the pottery found throughout Japan that had cords pressed into the clay to produce patterns. Although the Jomon Period stretched from around 10,000 until 300 BCE, it went through several different phases and there was a great deal of regional variation.

VILLAGE LIFE

The first villages in West Asia were small. Basic crops were wheat and barley, and domesticated animals included sheep, goats, pigs, and cattle, as well as dogs.

Farm life was hard, and at the mercy of the weather. But if successful, for the first time it allowed a large population to grow and be fed. The society could then support "specialists" such as stone-masons, weavers, traders, potters, or artists.

MILLET AND RICE

Neolithic China had several interesting cultures. On the Yellow River (Huang He) north of the modern city of Wuyang in Henan Province, the settlement of Jiahu covered a large area of 592,000 square feet (55,000 square meters) surrounded by a moat. Founded around 7000 BCE, the village was abandoned after a flood around 5700 BCE.

One of the earliest signs of the development of writing was found at Jiahu in the form of symbols carved on tortoise shells and bones. Thirty-three flutes found there, made from the wing bones of cranes, are the world's oldest playable musical instruments, and as well as pottery and turquoise carvings, the site offered evidence of the cultivation of millet and rice, and wine brewed from fermented rice, mixed with hawthorn leaves and honey.

Millet was a particularly useful crop since it grows quickly and provides a large harvest.

Like Jiahu, the village of Banpo was surrounded by a moat and contained symbols, this time on pottery. Dating to about 6800 BCE, Banpo was also in the Yellow River Valley, near Xian, and was part of the Yangshao Culture.

Millet, rice, and sorghum were cultivated, and possibly also the silkworm, but Banpo is best known for its fine black, white, and red pottery, usually painted with geometric designs, animals, or human faces. Children were buried in large, painted pottery jars.

In the east of China the culture known as Longshan was also known for its fine pottery, in this case distinctive black pieces.

THE SPREAD OF IDEAS

One of the best-preserved prehistoric sites in the eastern Mediterranean is also one of the most significant. At the village of Choirokoitia (Khirokitia) in southern Cyprus, people from the Near East mainland built a village in the 7th millennium BCE, bringing their new ideas of farming and permanent settlements. From the island these revolutionary Neolithic ideas then spread to Europe.

Choirokoitia contained circular, flat-roofed houses made from mud bricks and stone, each with a small, central courtyard surrounded by circular rooms or buildings. Hearths and basins were built into the houses, which were shared with the dead: bodies were buried in pits beneath the houses.

Bone, flint, and stone were all used by the people of Choirokoitia, who, although they did not make pottery, did make small figurines, mainly out of stone. As well as growing cereal crops, they kept pigs, sheep, and goats, while also gathering olives, nuts, and fruits, and hunting deer.

Choirokoitia was a developed, well-organized society, as shown by the defensive wall that encircled the village. Nearly 10 feet (3 m) high and built of stone, the wall helped the village survive for about 1,000 years until it was abandoned, for reasons unknown, in the 4th millennium BCE.

Reconstruction of Neolithic huts, Choirokoitia, Cyprus.

The region where the world's oldest civilization developed, the name Mesopotamia comes from the Greek words *mesos* meaning "middle" and *potamos* meaning "river." The two rivers were the Tigris and Euphrates in modern Iraq, and although this is where the ancient civilizations were centered, Mesopotamia in general was a broader region spreading into most of Iraq as well as parts of Syria and Turkey.

There was no one single, linear development of civilizations in the region. Cities and cultures overlapped with each other for long periods before one or other became dominant or fell, but broadly, ancient Mesopotamia was dominated by the Sumerians, followed by the Akkadians, then the Babylonians, the Assyrians, then finally the Persians before the Islamic empires introduced the Middle Ages in the region.

There is no one single reason why Mesopotamia became this "cradle of civilization." It is possible that with not one, but two rivers providing fertile flood plains, when the early farmers of the Fertile Crescent developed irrigation techniques, they were able to produce such a surplus of food that a complex society could arise. With the rulers of each area controlling the food and water supplies, they could organize the building of city walls, temples, and even more irrigation projects. Another feature of Mesopotamian societies was frequent, and often brutal, warfare.

SUMER, THE CIVILIZED LAND

"The Civilized Land" – Kengir – was the name the Sumerians gave to their country in southern Mesopotamia, or Sumer. This part of the region consisted of flat floodplains, turning into marshy reed swamps in the far south. Extremely fertile, once the Sumerians had built dikes to protect against the river overflowing its low banks, drains to empty the marshes, and channels for irrigation, they found themselves sitting on farmland that could supply barley, wheat, sesame, dates, onions, melons, figs, cucumbers and more.

Or rather, the Sumerian settlements plural stood upon the land. To protect against flood, their homes were built on raised reed and clay platforms, and their most important buildings, the temples, were also sited on mounds. Sumeria was a civilization built on clay: stone and wood were rare in southern Mesopotamia.

Some time in the 4th millennium BCE the first cities arose in Sumeria as many small settlements coalesced into larger ones plural, with the earliest cities being Eridu, Uruk, Bad-tibera, Nippur, and Kush.

A ROUGH GUIDE TO THE MAIN RULING POWERS IN MESOPOTAMIA

Sumerian City-States	c.3500
Akkadian Empire	c.2300
Sumerian Renaissance/Ur III	c.2112
Elam	c.2000
Babylonian Empire	c.1894
Kassites (Middle Babylonia)	c.1595
Assyrian Empire	c.1340
Neo-Assyrian Empire	c.911
Neo-Babylonian Empire	c.626
Persian Rule	c.539

The Land Between Two Rivers

Early city-life featured:

- a palace for the ruler
- a central ziggurat or mound for the main temple
- many other temples
- large public buildings
- separate residential areas
- narrow winding streets
- agriculture, fishing, stock-breeding, and cultivation of date palms to feed the population
- a centralized food store
- specialized artists and craftsmen such as potters, carpenters, smiths, seal engravers
- administrative records in the form of clay tablets

3500 BCE The first cities in the world are built in Mesopotamia: Eridu, Uruk, Ur, Larsa, Isin, Adab, Kullah, Lagash, Nippur, and Kish. They have intensive agricultural and irrigation techniques.

c.3500 The wheel is invented in Mesopotamia.

c.3300 The world's first writing, cuneiform, is invented in Sumeria, southern Mesopotamia. Written history begins.

3300 The domesticated horse is introduced to Iran.

3000 Sailing boats are introduced in Mesopotamia.

c.2700 The first person in "history," whose name is recorded in contemporary writing, is Enmebaragesi, king of Kish in Mesopotamia.

2500 Chariots are used for warfare in Sumeria.

c.2400 The first known female ruler is Queen Kubaba of Sumer.

Map of the main cities of Sumer.

CUNEIFORM WRITING

The most significant invention in human history since the development of agriculture, the world's first writing was found in the city of Uruk dating to around 3300 BCE. Created by pressing a wedge-shaped reed tool into wet clay, Sumerian cuneiform (which simply means "wedge-shaped") writing grew out of the pictograms that were inscribed on tokens that had been used for centuries in the region to record items and measures.

The pictogram signs became more abstract and were written in horizontal rows from left to right. Clay tablets could be reused if a permanent record was not needed, or could be baked in a kiln so the writing would be preserved. Up to 2 million cuneiform tablets have been found in Mesopotamia, and many of them only survived because they were baked accidentally when the palace or temple in which they were stored was burnt down by attackers.

Cuneiform inscriptions were also made on stelae and rock carvings, and with some variations, cuneiform was used by all the powers that dominated Mesopotamia until it was replaced by the efficient and practical Phoenician alphabet during the Neo-Assyrian Empire from 911 to 612 BCE. It died out completely in the first century CE and was a lost script until discovered and deciphered in the 19th century.

In this dawn of written history, the first person who name was written down by a contemporary was Enmebaragesi, king of Kish around 2700 BCE.

Sumerian cuneiform writing.

CULTURAL CONTINUITY

Although Sumerian dominance of Mesopotamia ended around 2300 BCE with the rise of the Akkadian Empire, there was a cultural continuity in the region, and all future Mesopotamian kingdoms inherited features of Sumer, the first civilization.

THE SUMERIAN KING LIST

Dating from the Old Babylonian period from about 1900 to 1600 BCE, the Sumerian King List is just what its name implies: a list of the Mesopotamian rulers from the legendary days of before the Flood to the 1st dynasty of Isin in the 2nd millennium BCE. Although it is an amazing historical document which has many sections that are thought to be accurate, the King List reports that before around 2295 BCE the individual kings each ruled for hundreds of years, and it also records that at any one time there was only one dynasty, ruling from a particular city, whereas archeologists know that there were dynasties contemporary to each other ruling their own cities or states. The king list is also flawed because it does not mention some important dynasties from Lagash and Uruk.

ZIGGURATS

Named after the Akkadian word ziqqurratu, a ziggurat was a tall temple tower built as a stepped pyramid. Reached by outside staircases or spiral ramps, the temple was situated at the very top. Trees and shrubs were often grown on the terraces and sloping sides (possibly giving rise to the legend of the Hanging Gardens of Babylon).

The Great Ziggurat of Ur was the largest of the many ziggurats built in Mesopotamia and even further afield, measuring 210 by 150 feet (64 by 46 m). Raised between 2113 and 2096 BCE by King Ur-Nammu, it was the main center of worship of the Sumerian moon god Nanna. First, up to 7 million mud and reed mud-bricks were used to build rectangular core mounds, which were then covered with a protective layer of waterproof baked clay bricks. Every six layers of bricks was strengthened by a reed mat, and regular, small gaps in the brickwork meant that moisture could evaporate from the core. Drains ran down the sides of the building to carry away rain.

The partially reconstructed Ziggurat of Ur in present-day Iraq.

SEALS

Thousands of seals, used to mark containers such as vessels, were used throughout Mesopotamia as well as Anatolia and Iran. In the north, stamp seals were more popular, whereas in Sumeria the cylinder seal was used. They were decorated with geometric designs or pictures of people and animals, and also identified the owner. Because the style of cylinder seals changed over time, they can be used to date any other items that they are found with.

A Sumerian cylinder seal showing a traditional boat used in the marshes.

Asia's second oldest civilization was also its largest. While the earlier Mesopotamian society covered about 25,000 square miles (65,000 sq km) and the later Shang kingdom extended into only a small part of modern China, the Indus Valley Civilization covered a massive 400,000 square miles (1.3 million sq km) at its height around 2400–1800 BCE.

Centered on the fertile valley of the Indus River, but also found in other river valleys, the culture arose in northwest Pakistan and northwest India, and spread to northeast Afghanistan, south to the Gulf of Khambhat on India's west coast, and southeast to the Yamuna River 30 miles (50 km) north of Delhi.

Sometimes called the Harappan Civilization, the Indus Valley Civilization

TOWN PLANNING

Agriculture developed in India by 8000 BCE, but it was not until large-scale irrigation techniques were introduced around 4500 BCE that settlements in the Indus Valley became significantly richer and larger.

The Indus cities were the earliest to be carefully planned. Instead of just developing in a higgledy-piggledy fashion, streets were laid out on a grid pattern, with straight "main" streets which would generally have had the appearance of blank walls, since houses were entered from the narrower side lanes. Different districts were clearly defined, so that the potters (identified by kilns in the buildings), or the dyers (identified by vats), were clustered together in their own distinct areas that were kept separate from other craftspeople such as those who worked with metal or shells. The cities had elaborate drainage systems, street lighting, and even some form of public trashcans.

Mohenjo-daro and Harappa were the largest Indus cities, each roughly a mile square originally, with populations at that time of 30,000 and 40,000 respectively. While this sounds like a large number, it still means that most people lived in smaller settlements outside the cities. Like several of the other important sites, Mohenjo-daro and Harappa were oriented

north–south, had a large, fortified citadel mound in the west, and a "lower town" in the east where most of the city's population lived and worked. At Kalibangan, another, less imposing, wall was built around the lower town.

In Mohenjo-daro the houses were very similar to each other, following a common pattern, and varying only by size. Larger houses were centered round an inner

MUD BRICKS

Mud bricks were the most common materials used to build the Indus Valley cities. Stone was used very rarely, especially since it is not found near Harappa, and timber was only occasionally used for some of the larger buildings and for flat roofs – sometimes as huge, square-cut beams – but plain mud was the main building material.

The bricks were made in an open mold, and were sometimes baked in the sun to harden them. To fit in special areas they would be sawn into separate parts, and, as is clear from the surviving walls and pavements, the Indus builders were highly skilled craftsmen.

was characterized by great cities – Harappa and Mohenjo-daro 400 miles (640 km) apart from each other in the Indus valley, Lothal and Dholavira in Gujarat, and Kalibangan in Rajasthan – that dominated the hundreds of other towns and villages in the area. Town planning, trade, drains, stone seals, and a mysterious script are other aspects of this first civilization on the Indian subcontinent.

3500 The first walled settlements appear in the Indus Valley.

2800 The Indus Valley people are using weights and measures with decimal ratios.

2400–1800 Height of the Indus Valley Civilization in northwest Pakistan and northwest India, and spreading to northeast Afghanistan.

770 845 024e

courtyard, or around several connecting courtyards if they were particularly extensive, and most of these larger homes had their own wells. The smallest houses consisted of little more than one space partitioned into living, bathing, and cooking areas, while some houses contained brick staircases, meaning that they either had two stories or flat roofs that formed part of the habitable area.

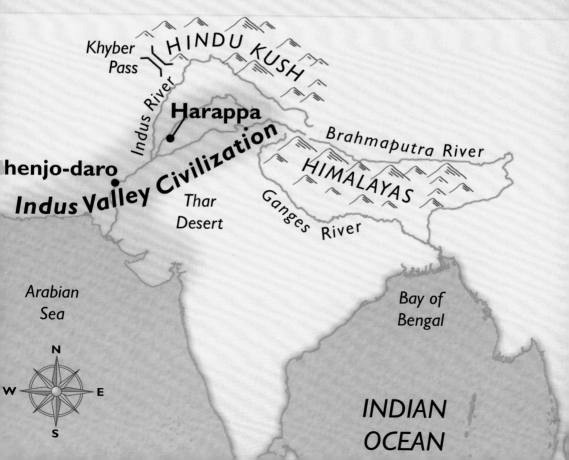

DOCKS, DAMS, AND DRAINS

With cities built close to major rivers, it is not surprising that the Indus Valley people were deeply concerned with water management. The defensive walls around the cities and the large platform mounds on which the citadels were raised are thought to have protected against flooding rather than invasion by other people, and within the cities there were complex draining systems. A particular feature of the civilization was its indoor plumbing. Even the smaller houses had separate bathrooms that were often more finely built than the rest of the house, and as well as washing basins, the facilities included toilets, with all drains flushing in water chutes through the building into the common sewers.

If houses were too small to have their own well, public wells were available in the residential areas.

Outside of the cities the farmers were focused on managing the annual flood that brought fertility by depositing rich soils and water upon the valley floors, but at the same time threatened crops and homes if the river overflowed. Several dams and reservoirs were built in the region, to divert water and then store it for irrigation. The city of Dholavira alone had sixteen reservoirs.

As a trading nation, docks were built in several cities, but the best surviving example is at the trading port of Lothal on the Gulf of Khambhat in west India. Made of baked bricks, the artificial dock is about 700 feet (214 m) by 118 feet (36 m), and at high tide ships could sail into it from the river (now dried up) through a 40-foot-wide (12 m) canal. As well as houses, wells, and streets, Lothal also contained a large warehouse, and was one of the cities that was defended against flood by a strong defensive wall.

The docks at Lothal.

THE GREAT BATH

Another unique water feature of the Indus Valley Civilization was the Great Bath at Mohenjo-daro, built in a central position in the northern half of the citadel. Made out of fine, baked bricks set on edge into gypsum mortar, it included a layer of bitumen or natural tar giving it a waterproof seal. Sunk about 8 feet (2.5 m) lower than the surrounding pavement, the Great Bath was 39 feet (12 m) long, 23 feet (7 m) wide, up to 79 feet (24 m) deep, and covered 897 square feet (83 sq m).

A sophisticated yet mysterious structure, the Great Bath was filled from a large well in an adjacent room, and a drainage outlet in one corner directed the waste water to the west side of the citadel mound. Steps, originally covered with timber treads set in bitumen, led down into the bath from either end, and around the bath were galleries and rooms that have been interpreted as changing rooms. Nearby was a set of bathrooms.

Although no one can be certain what the Great Bath was used for, it is assumed that it was a place for ritual bathing or other religious ceremonies.

The Great Bath in Mohenjo-daro.

AN UNKNOWN SCRIPT

Unlike the early Mesopotamian civilizations, we do not know the name of any individual from the Indus Valley cities. We do not know their legends or their history, their philosophy or what they thought of the foreigners they came into contact with.

This is because the Indus Valley script is too enigmatic to be deciphered. Known mainly from the seals, there are about 420 different pictograms so far identified, too many for an alphabet, so perhaps each symbol represented a word or a syllable, or maybe even an idea. The script is tentatively thought to be related to Dravidian, a family of languages that is mainly spoken in south India, but even that vague suggestion is hotly debated. At the moment, we simply cannot read the messages the Indus Valley people sent to each other.

THE INDUS VALLEY CIVILIZATION

THE FIRST LONG-DISTANCE TRADE

Some time around 3000 BCE what is thought to be the earliest long-distance trading network developed between the Indus Valley and Mesopotamia, where a colony of Indus merchants was eventually established. Only luxury goods were worth transporting such vast distances – precious metals, mineral, and stones, rare spices, and, later on, materials such as silk.

At its height, the Indus Valley Civilization imported painted pottery from Mesopotamia, turquoise from Persia, gold, silver, and lapis lazuli from Afghanistan, a jade-like stone from southern India, and all sorts of metals and minerals from northern India.

For shorter consignments, the agriculturally prosperous civilization appears to have exported surplus grain, making it richer and richer. Weights and measures were standardized throughout the region, and the Indus people were among the earliest to use decimal ratios in their measures.

THE INDUS SEALS

The Indus Valley Civilization is also known for its unique, mysterious stone seals. Nearly 4,000 have been discovered, most about 1 inch (2.54 cm) square, carved out of soapstone (steatite), then baked to harden them. Many have a knob at the back which might have been a handle, sometimes with a hole that may have been for a carrying cord, and most show a series of pictograms, or picture-like symbols, along with an animal: human or god figures are much rarer. One very common animal was mythological – the unicorn, the first depiction of unicorns in the world. Possibly images of this fantastic animal spread from the Indus Valley though Mesopotamia to the Classical world of Europe.

It is thought that the seals were used by merchants as stamps to mark consignments of goods. Certainly trade was a vital part of the culture, with Seals from Mohenjo-daro. *trading outposts established outside the Indus system westwards along the southern coast of Asia.*

FARMING IN THE INDUS VALLEY

Agriculture was the main occupation of ordinary people. As a Bronze Age society, bronze as well as copper was used for weapons and tools such as sickles and plows to help grow crops such as wheat, barley, millet, peas, and sesame. Dates were eaten, although we don't know if they were cultivated, and the Indus Valley supplies some of the earliest evidence of cotton being grown. Since a great many spindles were found along with a scrap of dyed cotton,

it seems the cotton was used for cloth. The presence of needles shows that material was stitched into clothing, and the people also had buttons made of shell, although they seem to have been used as ornaments.

Among the domesticated animals known to the Indus Valley were Asian elephants, whose tusks were widely used for art and tools. Other domesticated animals included cattle, poultry, cats and dogs, and possibly camels, buffaloes, and pigs.

INDUS VALLEY ARTS AND CRAFTS

Indus Valley craftsmen and -women used a wide range of materials: ivory, stone, metals, terracotta, and red pottery. The potter's wheel was used at the height of the civilization, and pots of all shapes and sizes have been found in the cities. The reddish-brown clay was baked and glazed, and was often decorated with geometric designs or animal motifs.

The Indus people spun yarn and wove cloth, and another major occupation at the time was jewelry-making. Ornaments of all sorts were made out of metals, bone, shells, and ivory, and their popularity is highlighted by the statuette from Mohenjo-daro known as the Dancing Girl. With her left hand on her hip and her right hand and foot raised, the Dancing Girl has an elaborate hairstyle, and wears a necklace, anklets, and dozens of bangles, most apparently made from shell. She boasted 4 bangles on her right arm, and 24 or 25 on her left arm, practically covering the whole limb.

Cast in bronze, the Dancing Girl shows the artistic skills of the Indus Valley. Most Indus statues were mainly small, as is another dancing figure, the limestone torso of a dancing man from Harappa. Stone was not found naturally near Harappa, so had to be imported at great cost and trouble, but the city considered it

The Dancing Girl statuette from Mohenjo-daro.

worth the effort to let the artist work with this valuable material.

Children were not neglected by the artists. Tiny carts and other toys such as bird-shaped whistles and clay monkeys that could slide down strings were similar to those found today in the subcontinent.

Although the Indus people worked hard at their agriculture and building works, they clearly had time to enjoy themselves and appreciate the finer things of life.

RELIGION

Apart from various god-forms carved on the seals, all the Indus cities contained a great many small terracotta figures of what are thought to be a fertility goddess. Wearing a necklace and a fan-shaped headdress, the woman is always shown standing upright, sometimes with a girdle or loincloth.

There is very little evidence of public places of worship, however. Archeologists assume the Great Bath was used for ritual purposes, and some temples containing what appear to be ritual objects have also been tentatively identified, but there are no clear signs of a priesthood, and like so much else, Harappan religion remains a mystery.

OTHER BUILDINGS

Apart from houses and working areas, the Indus cities contained several non-residential buildings whose purposes can only be guessed at. On the citadel mound to the west of Mohenjo-daro's Great Bath is a group of brick platforms about 5 feet (1.5 m) high which were once thought to form the base of a great granary, with what may have been brick loading bays. While granaries for storing wheat and barley have been definitely been identified in the Indus cities, some archeologists now believe that this "Great Granary" in Mohenjo-daro was actually just a large public meeting hall.

There are rooms that are thought to have been used by the administrators of the city and state, perhaps "government" officials or priests, and others that seem to have had some sort of ritual purpose. Mohenjo-daro's citadel also contained a rectangular hall containing four rows of vanished wooden columns, resting on the brick plinths that have survived in the hall. In a room next to this a stone statue of a man was found. Wearing an ornate headband, a matching armband, and a decorated cloak, he has a carefully trimmed beard, and in the absence of any other sign of a ruler, he is often referred to as the "Priest-King" of Mohenjo-daro.

A statue from the Indus Valley Civilization.

WHO DESTROYED THE INDUS VALLEY CITIES?

Some time between 1500 and 1200 BCE the oldest part of the Hindu Rig Veda was written down in Sanskrit, an Indo-European language. This collection of hymns and other spiritual writings reflected the traditions of a people calling themselves Aryans, who, it is thought, invaded India from the north. (This invasion theory is disputed by some academics today, who believe the Aryans may have been indigenous.) The chief deity acknowledged in the Rig Veda is Indra, the god of war among other attributes, who was credited by the invaders for helping them break down their enemies' "walled cities" and destroy their enemies' forts "as age eats a garment."

So Indian literature matches the archeological record, suggesting that the raiders administered the final deathblow to the already declining Indus Valley Civilization.

THE FALL OF THE CITIES

In the late second millennium BCE, raiders from the north swept through the Indus Valley cities, bringing a wave of destruction before moving on. In Mohenjo-daro the catastrophe was sudden and complete: bodies were left lying in the street to be discovered by archeologists thousands of years later.

Mohenjo-daro had often been in trouble. The city was flooded at least twice, despite its flood defenses, and even before the sudden attack that destroyed it, the city had become poorer and seemed to be in decline, with international trade ending and buildings crumbling and not being repaired.

It is possible that too many rivers dried up or changed their course so that previously rich agricultural land dried up. Another theory is that the land simply became degraded and could no longer support an urban population. Alternatively, perhaps there was one final, catastrophic flood. For whatever reason, by the time the invaders ravaged the area, the once magnificent civilization was already collapsing. By 1750 BCE the age of ancient urbanization was over in India. A small settlement remained in Harappa, in the southern part of the civilization there was some cultural continuity and folk memory recalled a distant age of greatness, but the impressive cities were forgotten until archeologists rediscovered them in the nineteenth century.

AN EGALITARIAN SOCIETY?

One thing missing from the Indus Valley Civilization is any clear sign of a social elite. Some houses were bigger than others, but there are no houses that are particularly grand or contain wealthier goods than the others. So although the Civilization clearly had a high degree of social organization and state centralization, we do not know if it was run by a priesthood, a hereditary aristocracy, or indeed, a priest-king.

IMPACT OF THE HARAPPANS

Although the Indus Valley Civilization was followed by a time of relative poverty in the region, the enigmatic Indus people had a subtle and enduring influence on the culture of the Indian subcontinent. The boats and bullock carts found there were similar to those used in India today, there were ritual objects similar to modern ones, and an artistic emphasis on bulls, tigers, and elephants that was reflected in later Indian religion.

The Dancing Girl and other statuettes show that bangles and elaborate nose ornaments were important to, just as they are part of South Asian culture today, and the very style of the Dancing Girl was similar to that of later Indian statuettes.

Bathing, especially ritual bathing, was clearly an important focus of Harappan life, just as it is even now in India, but one small steatite object hints that an element of the Indus Valley Civilization not only survived in India, but actually influenced the culture of the invaders. This is a seal showing what is thought to be a god figure sitting in a yoga position wearing a horned headdress, surrounded by wild animals: a rhino, a buffalo, an elephant, and a tiger. Some archeologists see this figure as the original symbolic representation of Pashupati, an aspect of the invaders' god Shiva. Known as the Lord of Animals, Pashupati was also a lord of yoga, and although this interpretation of the seal is disputed, it is still known as the Pashupati Seal. In later times Shiva was one of the gods who supplanted the war god Indra, so perhaps the Indus Valley Civilization had the last say.

Although the Sumerian city-states fought each other viciously and at different times one or other of them was ascendant, many of them were independent until about 2300 BCE Sargon of the city of Kish embarked on a campaign of conquest and forged the world's first empire.

Parts of Anatolia, Syria, and northern Mesopotamia, along with all of south Mesopotamia including Elam and Babylonia fell to his empire. Sargon made Akkad or Agade his capital city, and southern Mesopotamia became known as the "land of Sumer and Akkad." The Akkadian language eventually replaced Sumerian as the common tongue.

Sargon ruled for 56 years. The fourth Akkadian ruler, Sargon's grandson Naram-sin (2254–2218 BCE), assumed the grand title "king of the four quarters of the earth," but the Akkadian Empire had to struggle with constant rebellions, and fell apart soon after Naram-sin's reign.

SARGON OF AKKAD (c.2334–c.2279 BCE)

The first empire-builder the world had seen, Sargon was renowned for his intelligence and military prowess, and is believed to have begun what is now known as the Mesopotamian military tradition.

What we know of Sargon is mainly based on legends written in cuneiform many years after his death. According to one story, he was abandoned at birth and cast into a river in a basket of rushes. He was rescued and became a gardener, who was loved by the goddess Ishtar. A comment in the Sumerian King List mentions that he was once a cupbearer to King Ur-Zababa of Kish. Another myth claimed that his mother was a high priestess, giving him noble birth.

Sargon's capital city, Akkad or Agade, which would have contained contemporary records of him, was destroyed at the end of his dynasty and has never been discovered, although it may exist under another name. It is thought that Agade may have lain on the Euphrates between Kish and Sippar.

Sargon's daughter Enheduanna was given the important role of priestess of the moon god in Ur.

THE GUTI AND UR III

Following the Akkadian Empire, people known as Guti, who probably came from the region between the Zagros Mountains and the Tigris, became the dominant force in Mesopotamia. They are generally known as "viceroys" rather than kings, and they did not have total control of the area.

The Guti did not remain dominant for long, the city-states resumed their power struggles, and under the third dynasty of Ur, known as Ur III, Sumeria enjoyed a brief resurgence as the Neo-Sumerian Empire between 2112 and 2004 BCE.

An early law code, the Code of Ur-Nammu, was created during this period, and although it was the last era of Sumerian control of Mesopotamia, many aspects of Sumerian civilization were adopted by the future powers in the region.

From the 21st century BCE, Amorites from Syria occupied parts of Mesopotamia, building the small settlement of Babylon into a strong city. But it was the Elamites from Iran who took control of the region around 2000 BCE.

Opposite: Sargon the Great leading his army.

A fragment of the "Ur-Nammu" stele, from the reign of Ur-Nammu of the Third Dynasty of Ur.

c.2300 Sargon of Akkad founds the world's first great empire, taking over city-states in Mesopotamia and parts of Anatolia, the Levant, and Iran,

2285–50 Life of the first named author, Akkadian poet and priestess Enheduanna (Sargon's daughter).

2200 Public baths are built in Harappa, Indus Valley.

2200–1600 The Dilmun culture thrives in Bahrain.

2200 An Akkadian inscription in Mesopotamia mentions trade with the Indus Valley.

2113–2096 The Great Ziggurat of Ur is built in Sumeria.

2112–2004 The Neo-Sumerian Empire (Ur III dynasty) takes control of most of Mesopotamia.

2100–2050 An early law code, the Code of Ur-Nammu, is written in Ur.

c.2070 The semi-legendary Xia dynasty in China.

c.2012 The Guti people take precarious control in southern Mesopotamia.

c.2000 Wheel spokes are introduced in Assyria, making wheels much lighter and therefore faster.

The Gutians capturing a Babylonian city from the Akkadians.

Often a thorn in the side of its western neighbors in Mesopotamia, the first state in the region that is now Iran was the Kingdom of Elam. The word "*elam*" means mountain in Assyrian, and since the Mesopotamians invented writing and historical records first, that is that name by which the state is now known.

Although the Mesopotamians at first only used the name Elam to refer to the land in the north of Iran by the Zagros Mountains, the first cities in Iran were built on the fertile plains between the mountains and the sea in the west of the country, and when they began to dominate the north as well, the name was given to the whole area.

SUSA RISES AND FALLS

The plains in western Iran were called the Plains of Susiana after the Elamites' main city of Susa. Although the Mesopotamians considered their

neighbors to the east to be backwards barbarians who were always carrying out raids into civilized lands, the Elamites had gold, copper, and timber, so the

IRAN/PERSIA

Although the country of Iran has called itself by versions of that name for thousands of years, it was known in the West as Persia since Classical Greek times. The name Persia derives from Persis (Pars or Parsa, modern Fars), the home territory of the Achaemenids or Persians in southwestern Iran.

c.2000 The Elamites rebel against Sumeria and take control of Mesopotamia as far west as the Tigris, as well as most of Iran.

2000–1200 Tribes known as Aryans (Indo-Iranians), speaking Indo-European languages, migrate from southern Russia into Iran and India.

c.1750 Hammurabi retakes the Elamite kingdom in Iran.

Mesopotamians soon turned their attention in that direction. According to the Sumerian King List, King Enmebaragesi of the city of Kish asserted control over Elam around 2650 BCE, and Sargon of Akkad took tribute from the kingdom from about 2300 BCE. Another important Elamite city was Anshan, and

Susa was an important city not just for the Elamites but also for the later Persian and Parthian empires of Iran.

41

the whole region was sometimes referred to under that name.

Some 300 years later the Elamites threw off the Akkadian yoke, and became one of the important political states in West Asia. Their sudden military and political supremacy possibly caused a wave of instability through the region as they expanded to the banks of the Tigris in the west, as well as controlling most of Iran.

Their dominance was relatively short-lived, and it was Hammurabi of Babylon (reigned 1792–50 BCE) who reasserted control over Mesopotamia and subdued the Elamites. For the next thousand years there was regular conflict between the Elamites and their neighbors, and at one point Elam temporarily seized from Babylon two important stelae, one bearing Hammurabi's Code of Law. The Neo-Assyrian Empire, which began to dominate the region from around 750 BCE, often blamed the Elamites (sometimes rightly) for stirring up dissent in Mesopotamian cities.

When the Elamites conspired with Babylon against Ashurbanipal, the last great Assyrian emperor, it was their final, fatal mistake. After a series of campaigns, Ashurbanipal sacked Susa in 647 and by 640 had destroyed the kingdom. He claimed he was acting to avenge all the insults Elam had made against Mesopotamia, and boasted "Susa, the great holy city, abode of their gods, seat of their mysteries, I conquered. I entered its palaces, I opened their treasuries ... I destroyed the ziggurat ... I reduced the temples of Elam to nothing ..."

When Ashurbanipal destroyed the city of Susa the Elamite kingdom fractured into small political states. By then, newcomers to the region had already made an impact in West Asia. Known as Aryans, these peoples from the northern plains moved in several waves into both India and Iran.

Bronze statuette of an Elamite god with a golden hand, found in Susa, Iran.

ABRAHAM

It is thought by some that the patriarch Abraham – a holy figure in the three monotheistic religions of Judaism, Christianity, and Islam – may have fled the fighting in Ur at the time of the Elamite emergence around 2000 BCE, and found refuge in Canaan (later Israel).

God's promise to Abraham.

ELAMITE CULTURE

Although the Elamites adopted cuneiform writing, their own language has never been deciphered, so what little we know about the Elamites comes from the records of the various Mesopotamian states.

The Elamite cities were ruled by priest-kings, who led secret ceremonies in worship of their gods in sacred groves, attended only by the priestly class. They had an important goddess figure, and their main god was never named, so was only known as "the Susian." Elam had a complicated system of succession, and for at least part of the time was matrilineal, with a king's sister's son inheriting the throne. Its art and architecture was also influenced by Mesopotamia, with palaces and ziggurats mirroring those of its neighbors.

43

The first great monotheistic religion, Judaism centers round the worship of one God, the transcendent creator of the world, who entered into a covenant with the Jewish people. The essential Jewish laws were given to them by God, who promised them the land of Canaan. Jewish laws are not just rules to govern society through ethical and social behavior, but a series of religious practices and intricate customs for just about every area of life.

Jewish law is known as the halakhah, a word that can also be translated as the "path that one walks." Throughout history, observance of the laws has set Jews apart from other peoples since they determine everyday matters such as what foods can be eaten, health customs, and hygiene practices.

The Hebrew Bible (the Christians' Old Testament), is known as the Tanakh, an acronym of its three divisions: Torah (Law), Nevi'im (the Prophets), and Ketuvim (the Writings). The most sacred text of all is the Torah, which covers the religious basis of Judaism and the earliest history of the Jewish people. Consisting of

EARLY HEBREW HISTORY

According to Jewish tradition, the patriarch Abraham was born in the Mesopotamian city of Ur while it was dominated by the Chaldean dynasty. He was summoned by God and migrated to Canaan with some of his family. Making the Covenant with God, he agreed to God's laws, including the circumcision of male babies on the eighth day after birth, and was told that his descendants would be God's people and would inherit the land of Canaan. Abraham is a patriarch in the two other great monotheistic "Abrahamic" religions, Christianity and Islam.

Abraham and his followers became known as Hebrews, "the people who crossed over." Their language also became

Joseph interpreting the pharaoh's dreams. After this, Joseph, rose to become a powerful advisor to the pharaoh..

known as Hebrew. It is thought that the Hebrews were a semi-nomadic, semi-agricultural people, and that the period of the Jewish patriarchs and matriarchs may have been around 2000 to 1800 BCE. Abraham established his claim on the land by buying a burial site in Hebron, and his son Jacob, later known as Israel, founded the twelve tribes of Israel by fathering twelve sons.

Possibly between 1800 and 1700 BCE Jacob's youngest son, Joseph, was sold into slavery in Egypt by his jealous older brothers, but rose to become an adviser to the pharaoh. When famine hit the Canaan region, most people, including Jacob and his family, were forced to migrate into Egypt, where the fertile Nile lands could still support a large population. There, Joseph revealed himself and was reconciled with his family, helping them settle in Egypt.

It is thought that the pharaohs of the time may have been part of the conquering Hyksos dynasty and that would explain why the Hebrews eventually ended up enslaved. When the Egyptians rose up against the invaders and overthrew the Hyksos, they enslaved them and may have treated all foreigners the same way.

the Pentateuch, or Five Books of Moses (Genesis, Exodus, Leviticus, Numbers, Deuteronomy), it relates the story of creation; Abraham's covenant with God; God's revelations to Moses; basic Jewish laws, and the entry into the Promised Land. According to tradition, the Torah was given to Moses by God on Mount Sinai, though it is now thought that it was compiled over a period of time by several different authors.

6th century the religion of the people of Judah comes to be called Judaism.

c.604 Babylon exacts tribute from Judah. Daniel and other Israelite youths are supposedly taken into captivity in Babylon.

There is often no archeological evidence to support the history of the Jews as related in the Bible, but many of the broad events are known to have happened.

JEWISH BELIEFS

The most widely accepted definition of Jewish beliefs was summarized by the medieval scholar Maimonides as:

1 *There is a God*
2 *God is a unique, absolute unity*
3 *God has no physical body – he is everywhere*
4 *God is eternal*
5 *God and only God should be worshipped*
6 *God communicates with humans through prophecy*
7 *Moses was the greatest of the prophets*
8 *The Torah was given to Moses by God*
9 *The Torah is complete and may not be changed*
10 *God knows everything that we do*
11 *God rewards the righteous and punishes the wicked*
12 *There will be a Messiah*
13 *The righteous dead will be resurrected*

EXODUS

Four hundred years later God sent his prophet Moses to lead the Hebrews out of captivity in Egypt, and sent ten plagues to convince the pharaoh to let them go. When the pharaoh changed his mind and ordered his army to recapture the Hebrews, God parted the waters of the Red Sea to let them escape. The Exodus possibly dates to between 1300 and 1200 BCE.

Led by Moses, the Hebrews wandered in the wilderness for 40 years, during which time Moses received the written and oral Laws from God, including the Ten Commandments. In this period, the Hebrews developed the seven-day week, with one day of rest, mirroring the day that God rested after creating the world.

THE ISRAELITES

When Canaan was partly conquered by Joshua and the Hebrews resettled the land, they became known as Israelites, the children of Israel. This may have happened between 1200 and 1100 BCE.

Originally led by judges, who were war leaders as much as administrative rulers, the Israelites decided to elect a king, choosing Saul, a successful military leader. He was duly anointed king by Samuel, the prophet and last judge, but although he won victories against the Israelites' enemies he disobeyed God, so was replaced by David.

Originally a small city-state built on the banks of the Euphrates river, then later spreading to the Tigris river to the east, Babylon was first ruled by Sumer to its southeast, then Akkad to the northwest, and then by the Guti people.

In 1894 BCE King Sumuabum of Babylon declared independence and established a dynasty lasting 300 years. The name of the city, Babylon, became interchangeable with the territory it ruled, Babylonia.

THE CODE OF HAMMURABI

The Law Code of Hammurabi.

Written in cuneiform on stone stelae and clay tablets around 1754 BCE, the Code contains 282 laws similar to the Sumerian King Ur-Nammu's code, compiled from 2100–2050 BCE, and improved the earlier laws of Akkad and Assyria. Babylonia now was home to different peoples with their own individual cultures and rules and, to prevent feuds, the Code standardized justice with the concept of "an eye for an eye and tooth for a tooth." Punishments were scaled according to social status. For example, if a noble broke a fellow noble's arm, the offender would have their arm broken in turn. But if a noble broke a slave's arm, the punishment was a fine.

Hammurabi called his Code "verdicts of the just order." It covered 280 judgements on civil and criminal law including cases from day-to-day life such as:

- *murder; manslaughter; bodily injury*
- *theft; embezzlement; illegal felling of palm trees; receiving stolen goods; robbery; looting; burglary*
- *abduction; slavery and ransom; slavery for debt; runaway slaves, and the contesting of slave status; the rent of persons, animals, and ships and their respective tariffs; offences committed by hired labourers*
- *liability for negligent damage to fields and crop damage caused by grazing cattle*
- *taxes; legal problems of trade enterprises, particularly the relationship between the merchant and his employee travelling overland, and embezzlement of merchandise; trust monies; the proportion of interest to loan money; family law*
- *libel; corrupt administration of justice*
- *the legal position of the female publican; the price of a bride; dowry; the married woman's property; wives and concubines, and the legal position of their children; divorce; adoption; the wet nurse's contract; inheritance; the legal position of certain priestesses*
- *violent bulls.*

KING HAMMURABI (REIGNED c.1792–1750 BCE)

One of Babylon's most prominent rulers was Hammurabi, the sixth king. When he came to power Babylon's star shone. He invaded southern Mesopotamia, reaching the Persian Gulf, and stabilized the region. He also established an efficient, centralized bureaucracy and taxation system. Babylon under Hammurabi was later held to be a Golden Age, and from then on it was held in reverence by the rest of Mesopotamia, becoming the spiritual center of the region. Hammurabi's famous Law Code is among the oldest writings in the world.

1900 By now many of the Babylonian mathematical systems are established.

c.1894 The city of Babylon declares its independence and becomes a powerful state in Mesopotamia.

18th century Probably the world's first work of literature, the *Epic of Gilgamesh*, based on earlier poems, is written in Mesopotamia.

c.1792–1750 Reign of Hammurabi of Babylon.

c.1787 Under King Hammurabi, Babylonia takes over Mesopotamia.

17th century The Babylonian creation story the *Enuma Elish* is written down.

1595 The Hittites from Asia Minor sack Babylon.

c.1500–c.1157 Kassites from Iran take control of Babylonia.

c.1157 Elamites from Iran defeat the Kassites in Babylonia.

NEW RULERS

The Babylonian Empire steadily declined until the Hittites invaded in 1595 BCE, led by Mursali I who overthrew the Babylonian king Samsuditana. This enabled the Kassites, sweeping down from the eastern Babylonian mountains, to take power and establish a 400-year dynasty.

Assyria pulled away from Babylonian control and set up an independent empire, occasionally controlling parts of Babylonia although at other times the two empires coexisted. Eventually, Elam in Iran, growing in power, conquered most of Babylonia and the Kassite Empire fell around 1157 BCE.

King Hammurabi judging a surgeon who has been accused of malpractice. If found guilty, the surgeon's hands would be amputated.

ENUMA ELISH – THE SEVEN TABLETS OF CREATION

Literature and religion thrived in Babylonia during the last few centuries of Kassite rule, most importantly the poem called the Enuma Elish.

Discovered in the destroyed Library of Ashurbanipal at Nineveh, the poem called Enuma Elish (or Enûma Eliš) was recited in praise of the god Marduk at the New Year Festivals in Babylonia. Containing 1,000 lines of Old Babylonian/Akkadian script and written in cuneiform on seven clay tablets, the poem tells the story of the battle between the gods and the creation of the world. With the discovery of other cuneiform clay tablet versions from Assyria and Babylon, the original story is now thought to date back to at least the 17th century BCE, *and provides an important understanding of the Babylonians' view of the world. There are also similarities with Hammurabi's Code. Scholars now realize that certain biblical narratives in the book of Genesis mirror the original Mesopotamian text and that the Jews living in Babylonia must have been inspired by the poem.*

Enuma Elish, the Babylonian "Epic of Creation," was written on seven tablets, each 115 to 170 lines long.

NEBUCHADREZZAR I (1119–1098 BCE)

After various wars, the second dynasty of the city of Isin in southern Mesopotamia came to power. Its most prominent ruler was Nebuchadrezzar I, who led a campaign against the Elamites which resulted in the rescue and return of a stolen statue of Marduk, the primary god of Babylon. The statue was returned to Ésagila in Babylon. Nebuchadrezzar I fought off Assyrian advances for many years.

For many centuries after Nebuchadrezzar I, the Aramaean, Assyrian, and Chaldean tribes fought against each other for control of Babylonia. The Neo-Assyrian kings mainly ruled over Babylonia from the 9th century BCE until its empire fell in the late 7th century.

THE TOWER OF BABEL

The Tower of Babel is considered to be the great Babylonian ziggurat Etemenanki, "Temple of the Foundation of Heaven and Earth," dedicated to the god Marduk whose shrine is on the top, and believed originally to be around 200 feet (60 m) high. The word "babel" is formed from the Hebrew meaning "confusion" and biblical scholars suggest it is based on a mistranslation, or perhaps a pun (the English word "babble" is derived from babel). In Akkadian the foundation of the words Babylon and Babel mean "gateway of the gods."

The Tower of Babel, painted by Pieter Bruegel the Elder in 1563.

After her husband, King Shamshi-Adad V of Assyria, died (811 BCE), it is believed that the Babylonian Semiramis, as co-regent with her young son King Adad-nirari III, restored Babylon and built a wall of brick around the city. The respect she inspired by her actions during her regency is noted on various statues and stelae. Semiramis is shown in this painting hunting a lion outside Babylon.

OLD BABYLONIAN CULTURE

MUSIC

Music was a vital part of people's everyday life and contributed to religious and ceremonial occasions. Thousands of cuneiform tablets have been discovered describing the uses of music in Babylon and wider Mesopotamia. These include references to the tuning and playing of certain instruments together with musical scales. Representations of singers, dancers, and acrobats as well as religious and magic rituals confirm the great importance music played in society.

Lyres and harps were often beautifully painted with scenes of deer, trees, and lions hunting gazelles or goats, and decorated with silver, gold, copper, mother of pearl, colored limestone, or lapis lazuli inlays. The sound box was often in the form of the head of a standing or reclining bovine animal. A royal tomb at the city of Ur dating to around 2500 BCE contained the bodies of musicians and their lyres, sacrificed to the king.

Silver and bone wind instruments have also been found in Mesopotamia.

THE EPIC OF GILGAMESH

Probably the world's first work of literature, the Epic of Gilgamesh, written in Akkadian in the 19th century BCE, was discovered in the Library of Ashurbanipal at Nineveh. Although the twelve cuneiform tablets that were found are not complete, fragments of the story were later discovered in Anatolia and in further Mesopotamian archaeological digs.

The Gilgamesh story was known previously as five poems written in Sumerian during the first half of the 2nd millennium BCE:

- *Gilgamesh and Huwawa*
- *Gilgamesh and the Bull of Heaven*
- *Gilgamesh and the Agga of Kish*
- *Gilgamesh, Enkidu, and the Netherworld*
- *Death of Gilgamesh.*

A tablet describing Gilgamesh's meeting with Utnapishtim, who, like Noah in the Old Testament, built a boat to survive a great flood which killed the rest of mankind.

The epic begins praising Gilgamesh, who is part human and part divine, a "great builder and warrior, and knower of all things on land and sea." In response to Gilgamesh's harsh rule, the god Anu creates Enkidu, a wild man who initially lives among animals. Enkidu learns the ways of city life and goes to Uruk where Gilgamesh awaits him. There is a trial of strength between them and Gilgamesh is victorious. Enkidu becomes the friend and companion (although "the servant" in Sumerian texts) of Gilgamesh. They then both go against Huwawa – a divinely appointed guardian of a cedar forest. What happens next is not contained in the fragments of the tablet that has survived.

Gilgamesh returns to Uruk and rejects the goddess Ishtar's marriage proposal. Angry at Gilgamesh's rejection, she sends a divine bull to kill him but it is destroyed by Gilgamesh and Enkidu. Enkidu has a dream where the gods Anu, Ea, and Shamash decide that Gilgamesh must be destroyed for killing the bull. Enkidu becomes ill and dreams of a "house of dust" that awaits him. He dies and Gilgamesh grieves for him. Gilgamesh then makes a perilous journey to search for Utnapishtim, the survivor of the Babylonian Flood, to learn how to escape death. When he finds Utnapishtim Gilgamesh is told about the Flood and where to find a plant that can renew youth.

Gilgamesh finds the plant but it is eaten by a serpent, so Gilgamesh returns to Uruk a mortal. The last tablet relates to the loss of objects called "pukku and mikku" – possibly drum and drumstick – given by Ishtar to Gilgamesh. The epic ends with Enkidu's spirit promising to retrieve the objects, but then gives a grim account of the underworld.

The slaying of the bull of Ishtar.

Standardized tuning within a system that consisted of seven different and interrelated scales was in use during the Old Babylonian period from 1800 BCE, but evidence shows earlier Sumerian antecedents. Interestingly, these seven scales relate to seven Greek scales that were in use 1,400 years later; also, one of the scales commonly used by the Babylonians is equivalent to our modern-day scale: do-re-mi.

Babylonians also played a game with an elaborately decorated board, dice, and counters. Unfortunately, no one has found the rules so that we do not know how the game was played.

LANGUAGE AND WRITING

Babylonia was always a multicultural society with many differing tribes, language dialects, customs, and gods with the same attributes but different names.

During the time of Sargon of Akkad, the Akkadian language spread across Mesopotamia to the Mediterranean Sea and the Persian Gulf. By around 2000 BCE Akkadian had taken over from Sumerian as the common spoken language in southern

BABYLONIAN TRADE

Few countries exist without the trade of goods and raw materials to keep the economy going, and humanity has enthusiastically undertaken this for millennia. Babylonia was no exception. Limestone was quarried locally, but no other stone was available. Hardwood was also rare – palm trees were not suitable for carving or as a building material except for use as rough beams. As well as needing building materials, the Babylonians were wealthy enough to import a wide variety of luxury goods.

Traders and merchants came together to form overland caravans that traveled great distances. Ox carts carried heavy goods, while donkeys, which can carry up to 150 pounds (over 68 k), traveled the rough plains and mountains that carts were unable to negotiate, some going east across the Zagros mountains into Persia, Afghanistan, and beyond.

Ships sailed up and down the Euphrates and Tigris rivers to enable goods to go to Anatolia, and passed through the Persian Gulf to the Arabian Sea and to the Indus Valley. Trading outposts were established in many countries.

Along with trade, the Babylonian rulers regularly dispatched diplomatic gifts and messages to other powerful rulers.

TRADE GOODS

Exports
- *Sheep and goats*
- *Fish*
- *Dates*
- *Horn*
- *Flax*
- *Grains including barley*
- *Vegetables*
- *Leather*
- *Nuts*
- *Cooking oils*
- *Pottery*
- *Devotional figurines*
- *Ivory carvings*
- *Basketry wares*
- *Jewelry*
- *Wool – sheep and goats*

Imports
- *Timber*
- *Metal ore*
- *Egyptian gold*
- *Arabian copper*
- *Persian tin*
- *Indian ivory, pearls, and precious stones*
- *Indian spices*
- *Anatolian silver*
- *Semi-precious stones*
- *Cloth*

Mesopotamia, but Sumerian remained as the language of written sacred literature. Around the same time, Akkadian divided into the Assyrian dialect, spoken in the north of Mesopotamia, and the Babylonian dialect spoken in the south. Initially, Assyrian was largely used but the Babylonian took over and became the main language in the Middle East by the 9th century BCE. During the 7th–6th centuries BCE, Aramaic began to replace Babylonian as the main spoken language, but Babylonian was still used for texts on mathematics, astronomy, and other learned subjects. However, it had died out by the 1st century CE.

Aramaic was the language of the wandering Aramaean people, who often caused trouble to Mesopotamian kings. It became widely spoken in the Middle East and Arabia, and had a simpler alphabet than Mesopotamian scripts. Tiglath-pileser III, who ruled Assyria from 745 to 727, adopted this alphabet from his conquered territory of Syria, and without meaning to, left a priceless historical legacy when he had older records rewritten in it.

A Babylonian priestess dispatching a trade caravan. Under the first dynasty of Babylon priestesses were allowed to engage in commerce, but were forbidden to open or enter a beer shop: the penalty was death.

According to Chinese legends, five immortal wise rulers introduced the key inventions that shape human society. Medicine, agriculture, writing, the calendar, and the secret of silk cultivation were all supposed to be invented by the Five Rulers.

These sages chose their successors on merit, but eventually Yu, who was chosen because of his wisdom in preventing floods, appointed his son to follow him, beginning hereditary succession and starting the Xia dynasty. Historians are divided as to whether the Xia is a genuine historical stage or whether they are just legend. But at one point, the Shang dynasty was also thought to be nothing but myth ...

THE SHANG DYNASTY

The first Chinese dynasty to be known through historical records was the Shang, whose king list was recorded on what are called oracle bones. Around 1600 BCE the tribal chieftain Shang Tang, leader of a powerful group, is said to have overthrown the last ruler of the declining Xia dynasty, and established a kingdom on the fertile Yellow River.

One of the most important technological developments of the Shang was the beginnings of modern writing, which they inscribed on pottery and bronze, but mainly on thousands of oracle bones. The earliest of these to bear a written record dates to 1250 BCE. Used for divination, an ox shoulder blade, or the shell of a turtle, or some other bone would be cracked with a heated bronze tool to provide the answer to a question, then both question and answer were written on the bone in pictogrammatic characters that were clearly the forerunner of modern Chinese writing. The Shang were organized and meticulous: the oracle bone would also contain the date of the ritual and the name and ancestry of the person asking the question.

Religious sacrifices were mainly performed to the Shang's most important deity, Shang Di (the Lord on High), and also to the ancestors. Often divination would simply ask the ancestors to approach Shang Di for approval for an action. The kings oversaw the divinatory process, asking the crucial questions for the whole community, such as whether Shang Di would give a good harvest that year, or whether the ancestors approved of a particular military campaign.

Also included among the topics of divination recorded on oracle bones were childbearing, hunts, sickness, weather, dreams, and general good fortune.

The Yellow Emperor, one of the mythical Five Rulers of ancient China. The Yellow Emperor was thought to have invented weapons, wells, and field systems, and to have improved clothing and houses.

2000 Both China and Assyria now have complex, large-scale irrigation systems.

2000–1700 Tocharian people from southern Russia migrate south, introducing the chariot to Central Asia. Their mummified bodies in the Tarim Basin, Xinjiang, China are known as the "Tarim mummies."

c.1700 The town of Erlitou is occupied in China.

c.1600 The first historical dynasty in China, the Shang.

c.1200 Chariots are introduced to China from Central Asia.

1050 According to tradition, King Wen of the Western Zhou people in China writes down the basis of the fortune-telling system and spiritual guide the *Yi-jing*, commonly known as the *I Ching*, or "*Book of Changes*."

1046 The Zhou dynasty overthrows the Shang in China.

THE CHINESE ALPHABET

The oldest system of writing still in use, Chinese written characters were first properly developed in the Shang dynasty (c.1600–1046 BCE), although some earlier cultures had used inscriptions that may have foreshadowed Shang writing.

Chinese characters inscribed on .a stone tablet in an old Buddhist temple.

Chinese is not an actual alphabet where the written symbols indicate sounds and a word is built up from different arrangements of the letters. Instead, each Chinese character represents a specific meaning. It evolved from pictograms, where a picture of an object represented that object, through various stages until the character bore little resemblance to a picture of its meaning.

A classic example is the progression of the character ri, meaning "sun." The Shang symbol was a circle with a dot in the middle. Over time this changed to a circle with a wavy line running horizontally right through it, then to a semicircular shape, roughly straight on top with a horizontal line running through it, then finally to its modern form of a rough upright rectangle with a horizontal stroke within the rectangle.

Another example is the character ren, for "person." Its pictogram was a rough sideways silhouette of a person. As it evolved it was as if the person was bending over, still in silhouette, until today it is simply two curving lines that meet at their tops.

Words can be made up by combining characters.

Since written Chinese can only be understood if you recognize the characters, they have to be learnt by heart. But the Han emperors took an important step by standardizing the characters throughout the empire. This meant the scholar-bureaucrats on whom the empire depended could read messages sent to them from far-flung parts, confident that the characters meant the same thing no matter which dialect the writer spoke.

There are eight basic strokes that are used to write a character, and the strokes should always be made in a strict order. Beautiful calligraphy was considered the highest art form in China, and is still a sought-after skill.

SHANG BRONZES

In the Shang dynasty, China was the most advanced bronze-working civilization in the world, as the kingdom made a technological transition from the Neolithic, or New Stone Age, to the Bronze Age, when people worked with bronze metal for tools, crafts, and weapons. Bronze vessels of all types are associated with the Shang, particularly huge, possibly ritual ones, often decorated with animal masks or monstrous faces. Jade carvings, pots, and jewelry were also made.

The Shang also introduced the basis of the Chinese calendar. The priests needed to know the exact dates for rituals and festivals, so from the earliest days they made astronomical observations and kept calendars.

Several walled towns and cities were established, and the Shang kings settled their capital at Yin (near modern Anyang). Using chariots, powerful bows, and bronze weapons, the Shang had a military advantage over other Chinese kingdoms, and kept a standing army not just for offense, but also for defense against nomads from the northern steppes. Most people, however, made their living by working on farms, which they were allowed

The bronze Da Tung and Xi'an Bao Bao (Universal Peace and Baby Elephant) statue in Portland, Oregon, USA. It was inspired by a Shang wine pitcher..

Bronze cooking vessel, Shang Dynasty.

Oracle bone carved with characters, late Shang Dynasty.

to own, but only on behalf of the Shang rulers, the real owners of all the land.

The Shang also owned slaves, many of whom were buried alive in the large pit graves of the kings. Some were beheaded. The royal graves also contained bodies of horses and bronze vessels. Nearly all Shang tombs were robbed, but one that was not looted belonged to the Lady Fu Hao, who died around 1200 BCE. A wife of Emperor Wu Ding and an important woman in her own right, Fu Hao was buried with more than 1,000 precious jade and bronze objects, and nearly 7,000 of the cowrie shells that were used as money. She was also accompanied in death by six dogs and sixteen servants, probably human sacrifices.

But compared to one of the Shang kings, Fu Hao would have been an insignificant person, so the riches and sacrifices given to a king must have been incredible.

Petrified tortoise shell with oracle bone inscriptions, possibly Shang Dynasty.

DECLINE AND FALL

The Shang set the pattern for many of China's future dynasties as their kings became weaker and less able. The last Shang king was an unpopular tyrant, and in 1046 BCE he was overthrown and replaced by the Zhou family.

57

Soon after 3000 BCE a warrior people known as Hittites, riding horses and chariots, moved from north of the Black Sea into Asia Minor or Anatolia, the Asian part of Turkey. They conquered the local peoples, and learnt to write cuneifom from the Assyrian colonies in the region. By 2000 the various tribes of the Hittites united into an empire that by the mid-14th century BCE dominated Turkey, parts of the Levant, and northern Mesopotamia.

Relief carvings were typical of Hittite art.

The Hittites were possibly the first people to develop the use of iron, perhaps as early as the 18th century BCE. While this gave them a military advantage, iron soon spread around West Asia then further afield.

KADESH: THE FIRST HISTORICAL BATTLE

This is the first battle in human history for which there are historical details about the tactics and battle formations. Up to 6,000 chariots took part in the battle of Kadesh (Qadesh), near modern-day Homs in Syria in 1274. The largest chariot battle ever fought, it saw Egypt under Rameses II (Rameses the Great) and the Hittites under Muwatallis II fight for control of the region and the vital trade routes that flowed through it.

Details of the armies and strategies are known from the "Kadesh Inscriptions," a series of wall reliefs and papyrus writings found at various sites in Egypt, as well as from Hittite records, making it the best recorded battle in the ancient world.

According to the Hittites, the Egyptians had to withdraw in humiliation from the walled city of Kadesh. Egyptian records, however, claim that Rameses forced the Hittites to take refuge in the citadel. At this point his forces were so weakened that he could not sustain a siege, and had to pull his forces out. In modern terms, it was a draw.

THE FIRST PEACE TREATY

The Battle of Kadesh had an important aftermath: the world's earliest known international peace treaty. Drawn up in 1271 BCE and signed by the Egyptian pharaoh Rameses the Great and King Hattusilis III of the Hittites, the treaty was written in both the Mesopotamian language of Akkadian (also known as Babylonian–Assyrian) and in Egyptian hieroglyphics. The two rulers agreed to end the fighting between their nations, to come to each other's aid in case of invasion or civil unrest, and to extradite political rebels.

Originally recorded on silver tablets (and now inscribed on the walls of the United Nations head office), this treaty helped keep peace until the Hittite Empire fell not long afterwards. It was cemented in 1245 by the marriage of the eldest daughter of King Hattusilis to Rameses.

With their capital at Hattusas (modern Bôazkale) in Turkey, the Hittites' first expansion was halted soon after they sacked Babylon in 1595 BCE under King Mursali I. Then, in 1450 BCE, the Hittites began a new wave of conquest, and under King Suppiluliumas their empire reached the borders of Canaan (present-day Israel) around 1380 BCE. This expansion brought them into conflict with Rameses the Great (Rameses II) of Egypt, who was then a young king attempting to expand his kingdom. The two empires clashed at the Battle of Kadesh in 1274 BCE.

1595 The Hittites from Asia Minor sack Babylon.

1450 The Hittites begin to form an empire in Asia Minor and Syria.

1274 Battle of Kadesh (Qadesh) between the Hittites and Egypt under Rameses the Great for control of Syria. It is the first well-documented battle and the largest chariot battle ever fought.

1271 The world's first known peace treaty is drawn up between Egypt and the Hittites.

1245 The eldest daughter of King Hattusilis of the Hittites marries Rameses the Great of Egypt to cement peace between the states.

1210 The Hittites defeat a Cypriot fleet in the first known sea battle.

c.1200 First definite use of iron, by the Hittites in Asia Minor.

1193 The Hittite Empire collapses, partly due to attacks by invaders such as the Sea Peoples and Phrygians.

CONFLICT WITH ASSYRIA

As well as clashing with Egypt, the Hittites also clashed with the Mitanni and the Middle Assyrian Empire, which eventually took over many of the Hittite lands. Around 1200 BCE new invaders, the Sea People and the Phrygians, attacked Hittite lands, and the empire collapsed into separate city-states. Hattusas itself, with its monumental rock sculptures, burned to the ground. The small, weak cities were absorbed by the Neo-Assyrian emperors, and the Hittites vanished from history.

HITTITE LAW

Known as the Code of Nesilim, Hittite law was less about vengeful punishment and often centered on forcing wrongdoers to make restitution for crimes. This involved making a payment to the person wronged; for example, the payment for breaking a free man or woman's arm or leg, or knocking out their teeth, was 20 silver coins.

Capital punishment was also included in the Code, though, especially for disobeying a lord or the king. The Hittites also seemed to be obsessed with sexual intercourse with animals: the Code lists punishments for intercourse with a wide variety of different creatures (having sex with a horse was not a crime). It even outlines what should happen if the animal makes the sexual approach!

Although restitution was halved if the injured person was a slave, Hittite law specified certain rights and protections that slaves had. For example, they could choose who to marry and could buy their freedom.

A Hittite legal tablet, written in cuneiform, with an "envelope" and witness seals.

Once thought to be nothing but legend, the ruins of the city of Troy — along with some fabulous jewelry — were discovered by archeologist Heinrich Schliemann in the 1870s. He then went on to discover graves of wealthy important Mycenaean Greeks from the time of the Trojan War. His finds included a golden death mask, known as the Mask of Agamemnon, who was the Greek commander during the Trojan War.

Before the ruins were found, the stories of the ten-year siege of Troy, of Helen and Paris, and of the Trojan Horse were known through Greek poems and plays, in particular Homer's long epic poem, the *Iliad* (Troy was known as Ilion to the Greeks). Although only part of the *Iliad* has survived, it shows us the Greek view of the universe and of the war – that capricious gods interfered in human lives and people were often puppets ruled by fate and destiny.

THE STORY

The short story of the Trojan War is that Helen, wife of the Greek king Menelaus, ran off with the Trojan prince Paris. The Greeks assembled an awesome invasion fleet, and besieged Troy to get Helen back. Despite fierce battles and several single combats, the Trojans held out for ten years and finally fell to a trick. The Greeks built a huge wooden horse, and then pretended to abandon Troy. Instead, their soldiers hid inside the horse, and when the triumphant Trojans

dragged what they thought was a parting gift inside the city walls, the Greeks leapt out during the night, taking the Trojans by surprise and destroying the city.

However, there are many additional stories that fleshed out the bare facts. The gods – who were very real to the Greeks and acted like people do, with feuds, favorites, and wars – created the backdrop to the war and effectively determined its course.

Greeks and Trojans fighting in the Trojan War.

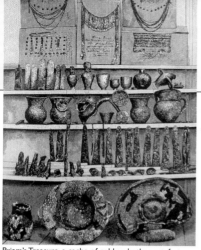

Priam's Treasure, a cache of gold and other artefacts discovered by Heinrich Schliemann.

c.1500–1000 Siege of Troy.

The Greek siege of Troy took place sometime between 1500 and 1000 BCE. Troy in Asia Minor or Anatolia was a wealthy, famous city controlling trade routes both on land and by sea through the Dardanelles or Hellespont. It was thought to have massive defensive walls, and according to legend had "topless towers."

THE FACE THAT LAUNCHED A THOUSAND SHIPS

Helen was also a tool of the gods. A great beauty, she was described by Elizabethan playwright Christopher Marlowe in his play *Doctor Fasutus* as "… the face that launch'd a thousand ships …" She had the choice of practically any single man in the Greek world to marry, and she chose the king of Sparta, Menelaus. But, Aphrodite decreed that Helen should fall in love with Paris and risk all by running away with him from Greece to Troy. Helen's brothers were the twins Castor and Pollux, who were immortalized as the star sign Gemini, the Twins. In Homer's story she later regrets that her action caused so many deaths, and in the end she is taken back to Sparta after the fall of Troy.

Helen's furious husband Menelaus called upon his older brother Agamemnon, king of powerful Mycenae, to form an invasion fleet. Some famous Greek heroes joined the army, including Achilles, who was invulnerable except for a spot on his heel, and Odysseus, whose ten-year journey home was the subject of Homer's other great poem, the *Odyssey*.

Helen of Troy.

61

THE JUDGEMENT OF PARIS

When the Trojan prince Paris was born, an oracle foresaw that he would bring about the destruction of the city. So, as happened in many stories, he was abandoned in the wild as a baby. He was found by a shepherd and grew into a beautiful youth, so he was chosen by the three goddesses Hera, Aphrodite, and Athena to judge which of them was the most beautiful. Paris was doomed from the start – he would win the favor of the goddess he chose, but was bound to offend the other two.

All three goddesses tried to bribe Paris. Hera offered him power and wealth. Athena promised him prowess in war and fame. Aphrodite, the goddess of love, enticed him with the offer of the love of the most beautiful woman in the world, and won his vote. He followed her instruction to make himself known to his real parents, Priam and Hecuba of Troy, then sail to Greece. But he won the enmity of two powerful goddesses, who supported the Greeks against the Trojans.

THE SIEGE OF TROY

On the plains outside the city the Greeks and Trojans fought battle after battle, although the Greeks could never breach the city's strong walls and the Trojans could never destroy the Greek camp or ships. The Greeks also ravaged the lands around the city, taking food, treasure, and prisoners, who were distributed to the chieftains as slaves.

There were often conflicts over women who had been taken prisoner, and in the ninth year of the siege, Achilles withdrew from the fighting for some time after he was forced to give his captive Briseis to Agamemnon.

A great deal of the *Iliad* is concerned with the internal conflicts among the Greeks, as well as with their funeral games and competitions for prizes. It also records the course of some of the battles, and details the single combats that took place. At many crucial stages the gods intervened to affect the course of the war.

The Trojans' great hero was the prince Hector, who was eventually killed by Achilles. Paris was guided by Aphrodite into killing Achilles, firing an arrow into his vulnerable heel, but soon after, when the Greeks were on the point of giving up, the wily Odysseus came up one last plan: the Trojan Horse.

The duel between Achilles and Hector.

The Judgement of Paris.

THE RUINS OF TROY

Incredibly, the archeologist Heinrich Schliemann actually used dynamite to blow off the top of the mound that covered the site he had identified as Troy. He thereby destroyed layers of archeological information, including probably much of the Homeric city, but he had indeed found a large, wealthy, well-built, and well-defended city that had at various times burned down. Among his finds was a cache of beautiful gold objects and jewelry, which he erroneously named "Priam's Treasure" and the "Jewels of Helen."

The Trojan Horse.

Ruins of the city of Troy.

The raiders who destroyed the Indus Valley cities around 1700 BCE probably originally came from the southern Russian and Central Asian steppes and may have entered India via Iran. Speaking an Indo-European language, they called themselves *Arya*, meaning "noble," which gave rise to the name "Aryan." Using horse-drawn wagons and chariots, they enjoyed a mobility that was lacking among the settled communities they met and overran.

Settling at first in the Punjab, the northern part of the Indus Valley region around the seven rivers of the Indus and her tributaries Jhelum, Chenab, Ravi, Beas, Sutlej, and Saraswati, the Aryans were originally nomadic herders.

EARLY VEDIC PERIOD, c. 1500–800 BCE

Settled village communities with pastoral and agrarian economies began to replace the nomadic life style. People tended cattle and sheep, and grew rice and wheat. Living in houses made of clay and bamboo, they used their chariots for racing and enjoyed gambling. Cattle was by far the most important commodity, and it is thought the early Aryans often raided other villages: the word for war meant "searching for cattle," while the word for kinship group, *me*, meant "cow pen."

Clan gatherings were common, including for the *yajna*, which was a ritual sacrifice conducted by the priest, performed to ensure the chief's valor and prosperity. A chief was selected by a combination of dice games, cattle raids, and chariot races, and received tribute payments in return for his protection. It was a patrilineal and patriarchal society, but women were respected and had some rights. There was no child marriage, and women could sit on local councils. A degree of social mobility was possible, as indicated by some hymns in the *Rig Veda*.

The *Rig Veda* describes conflicts between the Aryas and the peoples they met, who were called Dasyus, godless people. That word later came to mean "slave," signifying the relationship the conquerors had to the vanquished. During the early Vedic period the gods were seen as personifications of natural forces, and were worshipped outdoors in simple rituals performed by ordinary people themselves. The chief god in the *Rig Veda* is Indra, the powerful creator king of heaven and god of thunder and lightning, storms, rains, and the flow of rivers. Other important deities of this period included Prithvi, the mother of the gods; Agni, the fire god, and Yama, the god of death.

Sculpture of Lord Shiva at Elephanta Gharapuri Caves, Mumbai.

Between around 1500 to 500 BCE the oldest Hindu sacred texts, the four Vedas, were composed, giving the name "Vedic Period" to this time. The word "*veda*" simply means "knowledge." At first the hymns and other spiritual works were passed on from one generation to the next by being recited orally, but some time between 1500 and 1200 BCE the oldest

1500–800 Early Vedic Period in India. The *Rig Veda* is composed.
1200–1000 The three other sacred Vedic texts are composed.

part of the *Rig Veda* was written down in Sanskrit, giving an insight into society and life at the time.

Indra was also a war deity, and the Aryas gave him the credit for helping them conquer their enemies. In later times Indra was supplanted by Vishnu, Shiva, and Krishna when the worship of idols in temples was introduced.

Soon after 1000 BCE iron was introduced, meaning that jungles could be cleared with axes and heavier soils could be plowed for cultivation. Irrigation schemes were also developed, and the Arya people expanded southwards.

EARLY INDIAN KINGDOMS

Toward the end of the Early Vedic Period kingdoms began to form in India. The initial codification of the *Rig Veda* took place during the early Kuru Kingdom, thought to be from about 1200 to 900 BCE, although the dates of early rulers are a matter for debate.

Perhaps in the 9th century BCE, or perhaps earlier, King Parikshit of Kuru and his son Janamejaya forged the kingdom into the dominant political and cultural power of northern India. Parikshit is mentioned in the *Mahabharata* as succeeding to the throne of Hastinapur. He collected Vedic hymns into one text, as did Janamejaya, who also developed an important fire ritual during which offerings of food and drink were given to the gods, with the assistance of fire priests, in the hope of receiving a boon from the gods in return.

The Kuru state was conquered by the non-Vedic Salva people, and Vedic culture moved east under King Dalbhya, around 900–750 BCE, into Panchala.

Further to the east, in southeastern Nepal and northern Bihar, the Kingdom of Videha emerged around 850 BCE. Under its king Janaka (who is mentioned in the *Ramayana*), in the 8th or 7th century BCE the court hosted Brahman sages and philosophers. Janaka was thought to be an ideal king who, although surrounded by luxuries, had an attitude of non-attachment to material possessions.

VISHPALA

A female warrior named Vishpala is mentioned in the Rig Veda. *Vishpala lost a leg in battle, which was replaced with an iron one. This is the earliest known reference to a prosthetic limb, though some commentators argue that Vishpala was actually a horse.*

65

A map of Assyria and Parthia from the book *Geography* by the 2nd-century CE Greco-Roman astronomer and geographer Ptolemy.

Assur (Ashur), which was to become the capital of warlike Assyria, was one of the many Akkadian-speaking city states in northern Mesopotamia that were ruled by the Akkadian Empire of Sargon I and his dynasty from about 2300 BCE. It was a regional capital during the later Neo-Sumerian Empire of Ur III, and was dominated by its neighbours, the Mitanni, but a few hundred years later the region of Assyria in northern Mesopotamia had grown to become a major empire.

From about 1340 until the 7th century BCE Assyria was the dominant power in Mesopotamia, rivaled only at

THE FIRST ASSYRIAN EMPIRE

Around 1340 BCE Ashur-uballit of Assur rebelled against the neighboring Mitanni kingdom and occupied north-eastern Mesopotamia. Squeezed between the Hittites and the new Assyrian Empire, the Mitanni faded from history. Ashur-uballit and his successors set the pattern for Assyrian civilization: war, war, and more war.

A relief from Sennacherib's palace in Nineveh showing Assyrian soldiers in battle.

The first Assyrian emperors no doubt felt vulnerable to their powerful southern neighbors, and also had to defend themselves against raids from hill tribes in the east. Assyria became a military state, adopting military chariots, introducing effective, armed cavalry around 1000 BCE, and perhaps inventing siege weapons such as battering rams attached to mobile towers. They also used ladders to scale cities' walls.

Ashur-uballit called himself "Great King" and was the first to use the name Assyria, meaning "Land of Assur." The king Adad-nirari I (c.1295–c.1264) was the first to write that he was called to war by the gods, a claim that other Assyrians would also make. Apart from the desire for sheer conquest, the Assyrians also went to war to control or open up trade routes.

RULE BY TERROR

King Shalmaneser I (c.1263–c.1234) employed psychological warfare, boasting that he had put out one eye of 14,400 prisoners of war. He also used a common Assyrian strategy of reducing opposition among conquered people by deporting large numbers into other areas of the empire. With an efficient and large civil one time by the Babylonian Empire in the south. There were several main stages of Assyrian history:

- Archaic and Old Assyrian periods: around 2450 BCE the first inscriptions by urban kings appear but the city-states were generally dependencies of Sumeria, Babylonia, or the Mitanni
- Middle Assyrian Empire 14th to 11th centuries BCE (c.1340–1076)
- Neo-Assyrian Empire 9th to 7th centuries BCE (c.911–c.605)

At its peak as the Neo-Assyrian Empire, it reached from Egypt and Cyprus in the west to the eastern borders of Persia, and from the Caucasus in the north down to Egypt and the northern Arabian peninsula.

c.1340 The Middle Assyrian Empire comes to power in Mesopotamia.

c.1263–c.1234 Reign of Shalmaneser I in Assyria, who builds the city of Nimrud (Kalakh).

1200–800 Most of Armenia unites as a confederation of kingdoms, called "Land of Rivers" by the Assyrians.

c.1076 The Middle Assyrian Empire loses power.

c.1000 Assyria introduces an effective cavalry force.

service (needed to supply the army), clerks and public officials would accompany the troops, ready to record and organize the spoils of war, whether people or goods.

The Assyrians' reputation for cruelty grew. Carvings on palace walls and stelae showing the horrors of war were meant to terrorize and discourage enemies, and had the desired result since often people would surrender rather than face them in battle and risk brutal retribution.

But apart from warfare, the Assyrian kings also enjoyed large building projects, and created magnificent palaces and temples, expanding and improving their cities. By the 1st millennium BCE the cities of Nineveh and Ashur were both wealthy enough to boast stone bridges over the Tigris river.

At the end of Tiglath-pileser I's reign Assyria and other Mesopotamian states were increasingly threatened by the semi-nomadic Aramaean tribes, such as the Chaldeans, who began to settle in more and more areas of Mesopotamia. The Assyrian borders were pushed back, and the empire weakened for a time.

After capturing and destroying the fortress of Arinnu, Shalmaneser I pours out its dust as an offering to his god Ashur.

From around 1276 BCE until 1178 BCE people living on the coasts of Egypt, Syria, Palestine, Cyprus, and eastern Anatolia were terrorized by a confederacy of seafaring raiders known only as the Sea Peoples. The Egyptian and Hittite reports on the raids occasionally mention the names of tribes that were involved in the raids or the territories they came from, but no one has been able to establish where those lands were.

It is thought that the Sea Peoples might have contributed to the decline of the Hittite Empire, but in 1178 Rameses III of Egypt destroyed the Sea Peoples' invasion fleet, and the raiders vanished from history.

c.1193 The Hittite Empire collapses, partly due to attacks by invaders such as the Sea Peoples and Phrygians.

c.1175 Philistines, who may have been members of the Sea Peoples, settle in Canaan. The word Palestine derives from their name.

The final defeat of the Sea Peoples by Rameses III of Egypt at the Battle of the Delta, 1178 BCE.

Originally a semi-nomadic tribe that often paid allegiance to the Shang kings of China, the Zhou seized control of the kingdom in 1046 BCE after the Battle of Muye. Their justification for this rebellion against the last, tyrannical Shang king became a long-standing belief in China: that emperors and dynasties ruled only with the sanction and approval of the gods. If a ruler was weak and incompetent, or cruel and corrupt, then the gods had withdrawn their support from that dynasty, so it was time for a new ruling family. So the Zhou claimed that they had a "mandate of heaven" to rule with the title "Sons of Heaven."

China's longest lasting dynasty, covering some eight centuries, the Zhou established some of the political, social, and cultural characteristics that were to be part of China for the next two millennia.

c.1000 The earliest poetry collection in China, the *Shi Jing*, or *Book of Songs*, is compiled.

c.1000 Kung fu is practiced in China.

c.770 The full 64 hexagrams of the Chinese I-Ching have developed.

c.770 Spring and Autumn Period of the Eastern Zhou in China.

770–221 Hundred Schools of Thought in China as great philosophies are developed.

500 An extensive trade network in green jade from Taiwan develops around the South China Sea, to the Philippines, east Malaysia, south Vietnam, and Thailand.

500 Chinese people adopt the name Zhongguo (Middle Kingdom) as the Chinese name for China.

500 In China kites are used for military communication: the colors of the kites signal coded messages. At night, they carry lanterns, and according to legend, giant kites are used to lift military observers on reconnaissance missions.

500 By now Chinese people are using the abacus for counting and making calculations.

ZHOU INNOVATIONS

Making their capital at Xi'an (Chang'an), the Zhou developed a new, feudal form of government. Landowners were allowed power within their own territories, but were vassals of the king. Other innovations included:

- the use of iron
- coins
- ox-drawn plows
- crossbows
- horse-riding
- roads and canals

During the Zhou dynasty large-scale irrigation projects were introduced, which improved crops in the North China Plain. Towns grew up and trade increased, especially since communications were easier along the new roads and canals. One of the most significant developments was writing, which blossomed from its earlier primitive state.

In 771 BCE invaders killed the king Zhou Youwang (King You of Zhou), and the following year the dynasty moved their capital to Luoyang in the east, beginning a new Eastern Zhou period. But the Zhou were fatally weakened, and feudal chiefs began to take more and more power for themselves. In 770 BCE the country divided into several small states – 200 at one point – an era known as the Spring and Autumn Period. The name comes from a classic contemporary history, *The Spring and Autumn Annals*.

A hard pottery jar with a grid pattern, dating to the Eastern Zhou period.

THE ZHOU – SONS OF HEAVEN

WARRING STATES

By 475 BCE the small states of China had coalesced into a handful of main kingdoms, each struggling for supremacy. This period of the Eastern Zhou is named after another ancient book, *Intrigues of the Warring States*, and was a time of chaos and violence. As its name suggests, wars were commonplace, and corruption, bribery, false diplomacy, and espionage were rife.

Slowly, the Qin kingdom began to overcome its rivals, capturing the Zhou capital city of Luoyang in 256 BCE and eventually consolidating the separate kingdoms into China's first unified empire in 221 BCE.

CREATIVITY OUT OF CHAOS

Paradoxically, the tumultuous years of the Eastern Zhou dynasty formed one of the most creative and influential eras of Chinese history. Some of the ideas first put forward during this period became lasting cornerstones of Chinese culture and government, and, even further afield, they affected societies throughout East Asia.

Because so many philosophies arose from the 6th century to 221 BCE, the period has been called The Hundred Schools of Thought.

The general Sun Tzu, author of the book of military strategy *The Art of War*, the world's earliest known military handbook, fought his battles probably for the kingdoms of Qi and Wu during the Spring and Autumn Period, while the philosopher Confucius lived in the Warring States Period. The chaos that he saw affected him deeply, inspiring his belief that there had been a "Golden Age," an idealized perfect period of history that could be mimicked through "correct" behavior and ritual.

A bronze spearhead from China's Eastern Zhou dynasty, 5th century BCE.

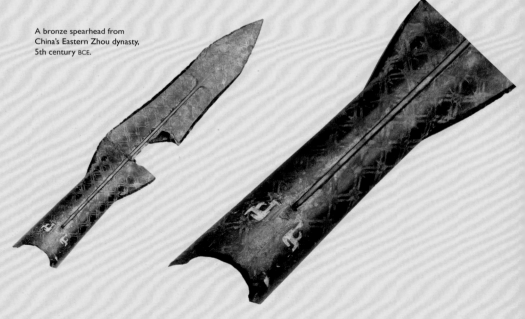

Sun Tzu's book of military strategy, *The Art of War*.

The Chinese general Sun Tzu.

Other Confucian philosophers such as Mencius and Xunzi also lived during the Warring States period, and according to legend, this was also the time of Laozi, founder of philosophical Daoism. Laozi is named as the author of the seminal Daoist text the *Daodejing* (*Tao-Te Ching*), and another important Daoist sage, Zhuangzi, also lived during the Warring States Period.

A third influential philosophy arose during the Warring States Period: Legalism. While Confucius wanted a just ruler, the Legalists such as Shang Yang and Li Si wanted a firm one. Concerned with creating a strong state through strong leadership, the Legalist philosophers saw their political theories adopted by the state that eventually brought an end to the Warring States Period in 221 BCE and produced China's first emperor, Qin Shi Huangdi.

Qin Shi Huang (259–210 BCE), king of the state of Qin who conquered all other Warring States and united China.

KING DAVID

David and his heroic warriors.

As a young shepherd boy armed only with a sling, the Jewish hero David famously killed Goliath, the 9-foot-tall (2.7 m), bronze-armored champion of the Philistines. Saul then made David a commander, and the young man became a close friend of Saul's son, Jonathan. Even though Saul become jealous of David's popularity and success and tried to kill him, when Saul and Jonathan died in battle with the Philistines David cried out his song of mourning, ending with: "How the mighty have fallen, and the weapons of war perished!"

At the age of 23, David was appointed king, based in Hebron, and began a golden age for the Israelites. A warrior king, he captured Jerusalem from the Jebusites, making it his new capital, and

THE WISDOM OF SOLOMON

THE FIRST TEMPLE

To house the Ark of the Covenant in Jerusalem Solomon built the first Temple, which quickly became the center of the religious and national life of the Israelites. It took seven years to build the Temple, and construction involved 200,000 Israelites as well as foreign workers. The materials used included stone, timber, iron, bronze, gold, and silver; tons of gold were used to plate the inner walls. The inside ceiling measured 180 feet (54.9 m) by 90 feet (27.5 m), and was 50 feet (15.3 m) high. In order to buy enough cedar wood from the king of Tyre, Solomon had to cede him 20 towns in the Galilee area.

Solomon's name meant "peace," and he extended his nation mainly by peaceful diplomacy, making alliances through trade and marriages. He was powerful enough to deal on equal terms with the great empires of Egypt and Assyria.

Fabulously wealthy, Solomon also quickly gained a reputation for wisdom. Just in case, he prepared for war, fortifying border cities, building up Jerusalem's defences, and keeping a force of war-chariots in readiness. He was famous for the administration of justice, and is said to have written 3,000 proverbs and 1,005 songs. His fame spread so that the Queen of Sheba, 1,000 miles to the south, heard of his wisdom and travelled to Jerusalem to consult him.

However, to pay for his luxurious realm, taxes were high and conscripted

c.1000 David becomes Jewish king.

961 David's son Solomon becomes Jewish king.

924 The Jewish tribes divide into the northern kingdom of Israel and the southern kingdom of Judah.

538 Cyrus the Great allows the Jewish exiles to return to Judah. The Jews return and build the second Temple in Jerusalem.

continued fighting until he controlled both sides of the Jordan river, the land up to the Mediterranean Sea, and from the borders of Egypt and the Red Sea to the Euphrates.

David united the twelve tribes, brought the Holy Ark which contained the Covenant to Jerusalem, and made plans to build a temple to house it. Up till then the Ark had been passed from city to city. A poet as well as a warrior, it is thought he may have written the Book of Psalms in the Bible.

His spiritual growth ended, however, when he fell in love with a married woman, Bathsheba, and arranged for her husband, Uriah, to be put in the front line of battle, where he was duly killed. This freed Bathsheba to marry David, and he promised her that their son Solomon would be king after him.

David's other sons reacted furiously to this decision. From then on his family was torn apart, with rebellions, rape, and murder. David may have ruled from about 1000 to 961 BCE.

According to tradition, the promised Messiah or deliverer of the Jewish people will be of his line.

labor was introduced. Upon his death, the disgruntled ten northern tribes broke away from the Davidic dynasty, ending the united kingdom of Israel. The northern kingdom became Israel, and the southern kingdom became known as Judah.

THE JUDGMENT OF SOLOMON

Solomon's most famous case involved a baby who was claimed by two different women. Solomon ordered a sword brought to the courtroom, then told a soldier to cut the child in two, and give each woman half. One woman immediately begged the king not to harm the baby, and said she would instead let the other woman have the whole child. Solomon immediately ruled that she must be the true mother.

THE LOST TRIBES OF ISRAEL

Israel and Judah separated into divided kingdoms around 924 BCE. Nearly two hundred years later the rising power of Assyria, under Tiglath-Pileser III (Pul), began to demand tribute from states in the region. In 722 the northern kingdom of Israel rebelled against the Assyrians but was crushed by Emperor Shalmaneser V. As punishment, the entire population was exiled, and the ten northern tribes vanished from history, becoming the lost tribes of Israel. Over the centuries peoples in countries as diverse as India, Ghana, South Africa, and Ethiopia have claimed descent from one of the lost tribes. More fantastical suggestions have been that Native Americans and Japanese people are descendants of the lost tribes.

With the exile of the Israelites, only the southern kingdom of Judah remained, populated by the tribes of Judah and Benjamin, and ruled from Jerusalem for 400 years by the line of David and Solomon. Known as Judahites, or Judeans to the later Romans, their name was eventually shortened to "Jews" and their religion became known as Judaism.

FOREIGN CONTROL

Not learning from the example of the northern kingdom, in 701 BCE Judah refused to make its tribute payment to Assyria. Under Sennacherib (ruled 704–681 BCE) the Assyrians invaded, destroying the city of Lachish in northern Judah, and besieging Jerusalem. Judah paid a ransom to save the city and acknowledged Assyrian sovereignty again.

Nearly 100 years later, after Assyria fell to the Babylonians, Egypt expanded to fill the power vacuum, and Pharaoh Necho II marched to fight the Babylonians at Carchemish in northern Syria. In 909 BCE his troops passed through Judah, opposed by the Judean king Josiah at the Battle of Megiddo. Josiah was killed and Egypt took control of Judah as a vassal state.

THE BABYLONIAN EXILE

In 605 BCE Nebuchadrezzar II, the greatest king of the Chaldean dynasty of Babylon, succeeded to the Babylonian throne. The following year he campaigned in the west, subduing Judah and supposedly taking several promising young people, including a youth named Daniel, back to Babylon.

Judah rebelled again and again, then finally, in 586 BCE Nebuchadrezzar reached the end of his patience and crushed the final revolt, destroying the Temple in Jerusalem, and deporting nearly all the people to Babylon. It was the end of the Biblical or First Temple Period and the beginning of the Jewish Diaspora.

King Nebuchadrezzar of Babylon at the siege of Jerusalem.

RETURN TO JERUSALEM

In 538 BCE, having conquered Babylon and taken control of all its territories, the Persian Emperor Cyrus the Great permitted the Jewish exiles to return home as long as they acknowledged his overall authority. About 50,000 Jews returned to build a second Temple in Jerusalem, but a significant number remained in Babylonia.

Nebuchadrezzar II in the Hanging Gardens of Babylon. The gardens were one of the Seven Wonders of the Ancient World.

THE LEGEND OF DANIEL

Daniel was probably only a figure of legend. According to the tradition, during his captivity in Babylon Daniel began to interpret dreams. When the new Babylonian ruler, Belshezzar, held a feast sometime around 562 to 539 BCE, the legend says that suddenly a hand appeared and wrote on the wall the words "Mene, Mene, Tekel, Upharsin." No one could interpret this until the queen thought to send for Daniel, who interpreted the writing on the wall as meaning that Belshazzar had been found wanting by God and that his empire would be given to the Medes and the Persians. The next day Belshazzar was found dead, and the Persian Empire took over the region.

Daniel in the lions' den.

Jealous courtiers then conspired against Daniel and tricked the emperor, who liked and respected Daniel, into sentencing him to death. Hoping for a miracle, the emperor had Daniel put into a lions' den, and just as he had hoped, God sent an angel to close the lions' jaws.

The biblical story refers to Darius, but seems to have confused the names of the rulers; the Persian emperor at the time was Cyrus the Great.

The Phoenicians of the Levant (Lebanon and parts of Syria and Israel) were notable for two things: they became great seagoing merchants, and they introduced the forerunner of the modern Western alphabet.

From around 1550 BCE to 300 BCE their ships from city-states such as Tyre, Sidon, and Byblos roamed the Mediterranean dealing in cedar and pine wood, metalwork and glass, wine, salt, dried fish, and, most importantly, their own Tyrian purple dye. This was

In ancient times, Phoenicia (present-day Lebanon) was known throughout the Mediterranean Sea as a land of traders

made from the *Murex* sea snail, and was so expensive that only wealthy Greeks could afford it. It became known as "royal purple." The very name "Phoenicia" derives from the Greek word for purple.

Their well-built wooden ships were single-masted, and their warships were armed with a ram at the prow. The Phoenicians founded the city of Carthage in North Africa, and may have sailed to Britain in search of tin.

Opposite: Phoenicians exploring Africa.

c.1200–800 Height of the Phoenician coastal city-states, centered on the Levant.
c.1050 The Phoenician alphabet, the ancestor of the modern Western alphabet, is developed.

Around 1050 BCE, they began to use a simple 22-letter alphabet, derived from Egyptian hieroglyphs, that became widely adopted by their trading partners. It was the ancestor of the Greek and Aramaic alphabets, and therefore the ancestor of their descendants Roman and Arabic.

Manufacturing "Tyrian Purple" in ancient Phoenicia.

From about 911 BCE the Assyrian kingdom began to fight back against Aramaean settlers, and to retake all the territories it had lost over the previous hundred-odd years. By 884 Assyria once again ruled all of northern Mesopotamia, and then under several warlike kings, it went on to become a huge, powerful, and terrifying Empire.

Ashurnasirpal II (883–859 BCE) campaigned in southern Armenia and Syria. He left a record of impaling, flaying, or beheading his enemies, and under him, the Assyrians began to fight not just to reclaim the territories they felt belonged to their nation, but also for prestige and loot.

Ashurnasirpal II continued his predecessors' great building works, restoring Nimrud and making it his capital. His palace there incorporated hundreds of limestone slabs with paintings or relief carvings, and covered 269,000 square feet (25,000 sq m). He boasted that 69,574 guests attended the opening ceremonies of the palace.

TIGLATH-PILESER III

After a short period of instability, the strong king Tiglath-pileser III (ruled 745–727 BCE) took power. He expanded into southern Syria, part of Israel, and the Zagros mountains, and took tribute from several small states anxious not to be invaded.

He carried out many reforms, including of the army. One of his major changes was imposing a more imperial system of rule, appointing governors to run provinces, instead of leaving local vassal kings in place. He left garrisons in key cities and regions, reformed taxation, and improved the system of royal messengers. (The Assyrians built good roads so their armies could march easily!) He also increased the number of mass deportations.

SENNACHERIB

Ruling from 705 or 704 until 681 BCE, Sennacherib was another strong king. Raiding western Iran, Syria, and Palestine, he boasted about the Elamites: "I cut their throats like sheep ... My prancing steeds, trained to harness, plunged into their welling blood as into a river; the wheels of my battle chariot were bespattered with blood and filth. I filled the plain with corpses of their warriors ..."

His greatest difficulty was with Babylon. The power of the Aramaean and Chaldean tribes there disrupted the Assyrians' safe trade routes, and although up till then Babylon had always been treated respectfully by the Assyrians, when the city stubbornly refused to accept Assyrian rule, Sennacherib destroyed it in 689 BCE. He plundered the temples and flooded the city, leaving it practically uninhabitable. Many Assyrians were shocked at this blasphemy, and when Sennacherib was assassinated, it was thought by some to be divine retribution.

In 701 Sennacherib made Nineveh his capital, building a huge palace there,

Nimrud.

911–605 Assyria reasserts itself as the Neo-Assyrian Empire.

883–59 Rule of Ashurnasirpal II in Assyria. He moves his capital to Nimrud and builds a huge palace there.

9th century Perhaps the first astronomical observatory on top of an Assyrian ziggurat is built on the temple of Ninurta at Kalakh.

811–06 Five-year reign of the only female Assyrian queen, Sammu-ramat or Semiramis, as regent for her son.

705/4–681 Reign of King Sennacherib of Assyria.

c.700 The bloodthirsty Assyrian army is about 200,000 strong.

689 Sennacherib of Assyria destroys the city of Babylon.

681 Sennacherib is assassinated by his sons.

668–627 Reign of Ashurbanipal in Assyria. He creates the oldest known surviving royal library at Nineveh.

659 At the Battle of Tulliz the Assyrians defeat Elam.

c.650 The first instructions for glassmaking are written in Assyria.

647 King Ashurbanipal of Assyria sacks the Elamite capital of Susa and destroys the kingdom.

627 Death of Ashurbanipal of Assyria. His sons weaken the empire by civil war.

612 The Assyrian empire fades as the Chaldean dynasty of Babylon and the Iranian Medes capture Nineveh, the last Assyrian city.

c.605 Battle of Carchemish on the Euphrates: the last stand of the Neo-Assyrians. With their Egyptian allies, the Neo-Assyrians try to fight back against the Neo-Babylonians, but are destroyed.

covered with relief carvings showing not just war but also scenes of construction projects. In order to bring a canal to the city he built an aqueduct that used about two million blocks of limestone, sealed with a type of cement.

Under Esarhaddon, who ruled from 680 to 669 BCE, the Assyrian Empire conquered Egypt and reached its greatest extent. Its last great king was his successor, Ashurbanipal, but after his death the empire soon fell to an alliance of Medes and Chaldean Babylonians.

Sennacherib on his throne before the city of Lachish (Lakhisha).

THE ASSYRIAN WAR MACHINE

At first a conscript army, with every man having to do military service for a year but mainly made up of farmers, the early Assyrian armies could only fight in the summer since the men would have to attend to planting or harvesting at other seasons. Tiglath-pileser III created what was in effect a standing army by bringing in huge numbers of conquered people who were available to fight all year round. From then on, almost every spring, the Assyrian troops mustered and marched to war, terrorizing the tribes and small states of a wider and wider region.

In the reign of Ashurnasirpal II the role of chariots changed. Previously, chariots were light, harnessed to one or two horses, and used as firing platforms for archers or for the general to gain an overview of the battle. The Assyrians developed heavy, four-horse chariots that could carry up to four men and were used

Restored entrance to the Assyrian city of Nineveh, near present-day Mosul in Northern Iraq.

A wall relief from Sennacherib's palace in Nineveh showing Assyrian soldiers wielding spears and shields in battle.

to break enemy formations, smashing into the infantry and scattering soldiers.

Cavalry also changed over time. At first two men would ride a horse, one to control the horse, the other an archer. Later, lancers rode solo, controlling the horse with one hand.

As well as mass deportations – in 703 BCE Sennacherib deported 208,000 people from Babylon – the Assyrians would sometimes salt their enemies' fields to deny them resources.

The worst treatment was reserved for rebels, who could expect the most brutal punishments, as shown on wall carvings and stelae. A quick death would have been merciful. Ashurnasirpal II reported the end of one rebellion as: "I burnt many captives from them. I captured many troops alive: from some I cut off their arms and hands; from others I cut off their noses, ears, and extremities. I gouged out the eyes of many troops. I burnt their adolescent boys and girls."

In the face of this threat, many people offered tribute to avoid the personal attention of the Assyrian armies.

Ashurnasirpal II with some of his prisoners of war. He was one of the most brutal Assyrian kings.

Ruling Neo-Assyria from 668 to 627 BCE, Ashurbanipal (sometimes spelled Assurbanipal or Asurbanipal, and called Asenappar in the Bible) was the last great king of the Assyrian Empire. Although warfare was a regular feature of his reign, he did not lead his troops into battle all the time. Instead, he is often depicted with a stylus at his belt, indicating one of his great loves: books. As well as magnificent carvings in his palace, Ashurbanipal left for the future the world's earliest known royal library, the Library of Ashurbanipal at Nineveh.

KING OF ASSYRIA

Like many Assyrian rulers, Ashurbanipal wrote autobiographical annals, which, together with a large volume of royal correspondence, gave a great many details about his life.

A younger son of King Esarhaddon and grandson of the powerful king Sennacherib, Ashurbanipal was appointed heir in 672, while his older brother, Shamash-shum-ukin, was only given Babylonia to rule, which made him subordinate to Ashurbanipal. Shamash-shum-ukin clearly resented being passed over for the throne of Assyria, and he was to cause constant problems for Ashurbanipal. Dynastic struggles were common: several of Sennacherib's own sons had conspired against him and assassinated him in one of the royal palaces of Nineveh because he had appointed the younger son, Esarhaddon, as crown prince.

The Queen Mother and King Ashurbanipal confront rebellious nobles in the royal garden.

Ashurbanipal himself claimed that he was chosen as heir to the throne because of his courage and intelligence. As the third son (the oldest brother died young), he had not expected to become king, so he had indulged his interests in literature and history by learning from scribes and priests. He was one of the few Assyrian kings who could read and write, not just Sumerian but also Akkadian and Aramaic, and he took a close interest in major building projects. He recorded that he had also studied mathematics and divination.

As a prince, Ashurbanipal was trained in statecraft, administration, horsemanship, hunting, and weapons skills. He was also given responsibilities at court when his father was away on military campaigns or diplomatic missions, becoming involved in ways of keeping the northern hill tribes under control, overseeing public works, and running the royal spy network. When Esarhaddon died in December 669 BCE Ashurbanipal took up the reins of power smoothly and was able to declare "I am Ashurbanipal, King of the World, King of Assyria."

He did however, have some family assistance. Before his death, Esarhaddon had arranged treaties with his Persian, Medean, and Parthian vassals to ensure they would accept Ashurbanipal, and the queen mother, Naqi'a-Zakutu, used her influence at court to ensure the allegiance of the royal family and powerful courtiers.

Assyrian scribes.

ASHURBANIPAL'S MAJOR CAMPAIGNS

- *Quelling two revolts in Egypt, sacking Thebes*
- *Pushing the Kushites out of Egypt*
- *Besieging the Phoenician city of Tyre, which had supported Egyptian and Lydian revolts, and winning renewed allegiance from rulers in Syria and Asia Minor*
- *Repulsing Cimmerian invaders from the North Caucasus*
- *Preventing advances from Arab tribes*
- *Besieging and conquering Babylon in 648 BCE*
- *Crushing the Elamites, sacking Susa in 647 BCE*

Wall relief from the palace of Nineveh showing Ashurbanipal during a military campaign.

THE WARRIOR KING

Ashurbanipal inherited the great Neo-Assyrian empire, and during his reign extended it even further into the largest polity in the world at the time, reaching from central Iran to the eastern Mediterranean and Cyprus, and from Cilicia in Asia Minor to the Arab peninsula. For part of his reign he even controlled Egypt. His capital, Nineveh, was the greatest city in the world at that time.

From almost the moment he took the throne Ashurbanipal was involved in putting down revolts and extending the empire. Although like most Assyrians he was cruel and brutal to his military enemies, he usually left civilian populations alone, and often appointed local princes to govern the conquered land. Kept in line by an Assyrian garrison, as long as the local ruler maintained allegiance to him (and paid tribute), Ashurbanipal ruled lightly. Following Assyrian custom, another tactic was to move conquered people, especially their leaders, away from their homeland and to other parts of the empire.

His treatment of rebels was harsh, though, and he proudly wrote about beheadings, mutilations, and burning

LION-HUNTING

Ashurbanipal's palaces in Nineveh contained many relief carvings showing the king hunting and killing lions. He boasted that "I pierced the throats of raging lions, each with a single arrow," and one of the carvings showed him strangling a lion with his bare hands.

Whether or not that image is true, the royal lion hunt was more than just exercise or entertainment. Instead, it was a symbol of how the king could defend his people from danger. So, by glorifying his hunts through magnificent art, Ashurbanipal was not just showing off, he was also showing how he could protect the kingdom.

Ashurbanipal was a patron of the arts. The many bas-reliefs and sculptures at Nineveh that showed his triumphs and achievements represent a high point in ancient West Asian art.

A relief from Ashurbanipal's palace showing him defeating a lion with his bare hands.

captives alive. About some of the persistently troublesome Elamite royals he recorded: "I killed them. Their heads I cut off in front of each other." In an otherwise charming wall relief in his palace, Ashurbanipal and his wife Ashurshurrat are shown drinking wine in a garden. But hanging from a tree is the head of an Elamite king.

Later Ashurbanipal went on to record: "I had the sanctuaries of the land Elam utterly destroyed ... I devastated the districts of the land Elam."

In at least one instance, however, Ashurbanipal withheld the might of the Assyrian army as punishment and a warning to other potential troublemakers. Invaded by Cimmerians from the North Caucasus, the Lydians of Asia Minor asked for Ashurbanipal's help, which, because Lydians mercenaries had aided an Egyptian revolt, he refused. The Lydian king was killed by the invaders, and his son promptly renewed allegiance to Ashurbanipal in return for military aid.

THE BABYLON CAMPAIGN

For 16 years Ashurbanipal and his brother Shamash-shum-ukin, who ruled Babylonia with restricted powers, maintained peaceful relations. It is also possible that some of Ashurbanipal's military actions in the south of the empire aimed to help protect his brother. But for whatever reason, Shamash-shum-ukin was dissatisfied with the situation, and attempted to organize a coordinated rebellion by people on the periphery of the empire: Egypt, Judah, Lydia, Phoenicia, Elam, and tribesmen from Arabia and Chaldea.

In 652 Shamash-shum-ukin rose up against his brother, but although he did receive some aid, a huge rebellion never materialized. Ashurbanipal besieged the city of Babylon, preventing further support getting through to his brother, and starving the population. In 648 the city fell. According to legend, Shamash-shum-ukin died in his burning palace.

Ashurbanipal treated the rebels harshly, whether Babylonians, Elamites, or Arabs. However, he did not destroy Babylon, instead restoring it and appointing a Chaldean viceroy to replace his brother.

The Babylon campaign and punitive expeditions against Elam were Ashurbanipal's last major actions. Although Egypt shook off Assyrian rule, he did not try to retake the country, and for the last years of his reign the empire was effectively at peace.

FALL OF AN EMPIRE

Despite regular warfare, the Neo-Assyrian Empire prospered under Ashurbanipal, who was an able administrator and a popular king to his own people, if not to his neighbors such as the Elamites and Babylonians. During the first year of his reign there was what was noted as a record harvest, and since at the time it was thought that such a bounty was a gift of the gods, this was thought to be a sign that the gods looked favorably on him.

But from 631 BCE there is little known about him other than that the last years of his reign were peaceful. We also have very little information on the sons who succeeded him after his death around 627 BCE and who seemed to weaken the empire through civil war. There were external pressures, too, as the empire had become so vast that the government and army were over-extended.

For whatever reasons, less than two decades after Ashurbanipal's death, Assyria collapsed and Nineveh, its last city, was destroyed by an alliance of Medes from Iran and the Chaldean dynasty of Babylon. Ashurbanipal was not the last Assyrian king, as was sometimes thought, but he was its last great king.

THE ROYAL LIBRARY

Temple archives were collected in Sumer as early as 2600 BCE. Both commercial and government records were also maintained at various sites in Mesopotamia, and it is possible that there were libraries at Nippur about 1900 BCE and at Nineveh around 700 BCE.

But the Royal Library of Ashurbanipal at Nineveh was the first known attempt to systematically collect, catalog, and store for easy retrieval texts of all sorts and from as wide an area as possible.

Ashurbanipal was deeply religious and believed in omens, traits that were part of the inspiration behind his library, since the largest part of his collection were "omen texts:" writings on divination, astrology, and ritual. But the library also contained medical and mathematical works, incantations, prayers and religious documents, dictionaries in various languages, letters, notes on government and social administration, proverbs, creation stories, folk tales and works of literature such as The Epic of Gilgamesh.

Another important text was the Flood Tablet, telling the story of the Great Flood that was otherwise only known from the Bible.

As well as gathering all he could from temple archives in his major cities, Ashurbanipal sent scribes throughout his empire to make copies of every text they could find. He was a true book-lover: whenever possible he had duplicates made, and many of the cuneiform clay tablets in the library had his own personal mark on them.

When Nineveh was destroyed by the Medes and Babylonians in 612 BCE, the royal palaces were burnt to the ground. Although the bulk of Ashurbanipal's collection was destroyed, incredibly, more than 20,000 fragments of texts survived, giving a unique insight into Assyrian religion, administration, and literature.

The Royal Library of Ashurbanipal at Nineveh.

DILMUN: A GARDEN PARADISE

Described in the Sumerian *Epic of Gilgamesh* and in some versions of the Sumerian creation story as a garden paradise, the trading hub of Dilmun on the Persian Gulf probably covered modern-day Bahrain, Kuwait, Qatar, and the eastern part of Saudi Arabia.

In the Sumerian story of *Enki and Ninhursag*, Enki promises: "For Dilmun, the land of my lady's heart, I will create long waterways, rivers and canals, whereby water will flow to quench the thirst of all beings and bring abundance to all that lives."

Ideally located next to the sea and freshwater springs that have since dried up, Dilmun then enjoyed a much wetter climate than today, and was a fertile land producing an agricultural surplus to be traded. At its height from about 3000 to 1800 BCE, the kingdom also controlled the long-distance maritime trade in the Gulf.

Pearls from the Gulf, copper from Oman, tin, bitumen, wool, and olive oil from Mesopotamia, and cotton from the Indus Valley Civilization, all passed

Ruins of the the Dilmun civilization.

2200–1600 The Dilmun culture thrives in Bahrain.
c.700 The incense trade route across land from southern Arabia to North Africa and West Asia develops.

through Dilmun, whose trading seals have been found in Mesopotamian cities. The link with the Indus Valley cities was clearly particularly important, since the weights and measures used in Dilmun were those of the Indus Valley rather than those of any other trading partner.

Much later on, from the 3rd century CE, the network extended to China and the Mediterranean.

Inscriptions in Assyria dating to 1250 BCE record tribute from Dilmun and claim rulership of the region. Sennacherib, king of Assyria from 707–681 BCE, attacked northeast Arabia and may have asserted

THE SABAEANS

Speaking an old South Arabian language, the Sabaeans lived in what is today Yemen in the southwest Arabian peninsula, thriving from around 2000 BCE to the 8th century BCE. With an economy based on the export of precious frankincense and myrrh, it controlled the Red Sea trade, and was powerful and influential. Some historians believe that Saba was the biblical Kingdom of Sheba. Saba vied with other kingdoms such as Himyar, Awsan, and Qataban, and as well as maritime trade, ran overland caravans with goods carried by camels along the Incense Roads, the trade route through Arabia to northeast Africa and the Levant.

Around 280 CE the Himyaran Empire conquered the Sabaeans and became the dominant Arabian state until about 525 CE. As well as spices, the goods they imported included ivory, precious woods, and even exotic feathers from East Africa to be shipped on into the Roman world.

dominion over the region, and a Neo-Babylonian record of 567 BCE also claimed nominal sovereignty over Dilmun.

From around 1800 BCE, Dilmun's commercial influence declined because of piracy in the Persian Gulf, and that name was not recorded after the fall of Babylon in 538 BCE.

Bahrain was claimed as part of the Persian Achaemenian Empire, and the fertile islands – and their pearl trade – were of great interest to the Persians' conqueror,

A painting representing Bahrain during the Dilmun era.

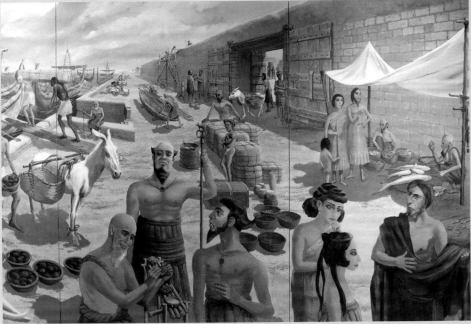

Dilmun-era exhibits on display in the Bahrain Fort Museum, Al Qalah, Kingdom of Bahrain.

Alexander the Great. He planned to settle large numbers of Greek colonists there, and although it never happened on the scale that he had intended, the region, known to the Greeks as Tylos, became part of the wider Hellenized world. The name Tylos may have been the Hellenization of the Semitic word Tilmun (from Dilmun).

EDOM OR IDUMEA

After the Jews were taken into captivity in Babylon from 586 BCE, the Edomites from Jordan took over fertile territory in Judah. Known from Assyrian records, they are also mentioned several times in the Bible.

The ruins of Avdat in the Negev desert.

From tiny statuettes and seals to large stone monuments, and from jewelry to pottery, the Mesopotamian

Relief carvings were common in some of the great Mesopotamian palaces.

THE WARKA VASE

Mesopotamia's oldest known carved ritual vase, the Warka Vase (Warka is a name for Uruk), is dated to around 3100 BCE. Nearly 4 feet (1 m) high, it has intricate carvings showing worship of the goddess Inanna.

The Warka Vase is a carved alabaster stone vessel found in the temple complex of the Sumerian goddess Inanna in the ruins of the ancient city of Uruk, southern Iraq.

A Sumerian stone wall relief carving.

A stone dating between 2005 BCE and 1595 BCE showing the Sumerian King List, written in cuneiform in two columns on each of the four sides.

THE STELE OF VULTURES

Carved stone slabs sometimes commemorated important events. The Stele of the Vultures, dating from 2600 to 2350 BCE, celebrates the victory of the city-state of Lagash over Umma. Made of a single slab of limestone originally nearly 6 feet (1.8 m) high, one side is carved with reliefs showing the actual events, while the other side shows mythological themes. This was common for many stelae of the time, although many temple stelae did not have any explanatory inscriptions.

Fragment of the Stele of the Vultures showing vultures with severed human heads in their beaks and a section of cuneiform script.

civilizations enjoyed ornate and complex art in all forms.

The main material in Sumer was clay, and much of its early art was religious, meant for the temples. Carved stone or alabaster vessels, religious stelae or stone slabs, and votive offerings were common art forms in the early period. Patterns of clay cones in different colors were used as mosaics to decorate temples.

Sumerian art often explored the natural world or the relationship between humans and deities. Although animals and plants were also common subjects, sometimes they were used to represent deities or religious themes.

From the early days clay cylinder seals were very finely executed, despite their small size. Other distinctive aspects of Sumerian art are statuettes with wide, staring eyes, often with hands clasped together in a gesture of worship or prayer. Men are shown with long hair and beards, and women with coils of hair. Long, pleated skirts are common.

THE ROYAL TOMBS OF UR

Excavations of the royal tombs at Ur revealed wonderful examples of finely decorated objects such as musical instruments, weapons, jewelry, illustrated panels, and statuettes. Materials used included gold, silver, marble, lapis lazuli, ivory, and shell, many imported.

The headless statue
of Queen Napirasu.

THE HEADLESS QUEEN

*The headless statue of Queen Napirasu of Elam is one of the most
extraordinary pieces of art from the era. Dating to about 1300 BCE,
the cone-shaped figure was created by casting a copper skin over
a bronze core using the lost-wax method, with the two parts held
together by pins and splints. Originally the sides would have
been covered with gold or silver.*

*The queen is shown standing, with her hands folded in
front of her. It is not the usual worship pose, and in this case
is thought to be possibly a sign of fertility. She wears a short-
sleeved gown covered with embroidery, a fringed shawl, and
several pieces of jewelry. The delicate details lighten what
would otherwise be a massive work – the statue is life-size,
and weighs two tons; the amount of metal used shows how
wealthy her kingdom was.*

*On the front of Napirasu's skirt is an Elamite
inscription of the queen's name and titles, as well as
an invocation placing the statue under the protection
of four deities and calling down their curse on
attempted thieves or anyone trying to desecrate the
statue:*

*"He who would seize my statue, who would
smash it, who would destroy its inscription, who
would erase my name, may he be smitten by the curse
of [the gods], that his name shall become extinct, that
his offspring be barren ... This is Napirasu's offering."*

SOUVENIRS

Just as today, souvenir items were
available from temples in the form
of small terracotta plaques showing
religious themes. These souvenirs may
have been copies of much larger pieces,
such as the "Burney Relief" of a naked,
winged goddess with the feet of a bird
of prey, that were on display in temples.
From around 967 BCE Assyrian palaces
often incorporated colossal statues with a
human head, the body of a bull or a lion,
and bird wings. Known as *lamassu*, these
were protective deities, a symbol of power,

The gold wig
helmet of King
Meskalamdug
from the royal
tombs at Ur,
c.2500 BCE.

and usually stood in pairs at entrances or
in inner courtyards.

Tiny copies were buried in houses for
protection.

PICTURE STORIES

Another Assyrian art form was the picture story, a series of pictures carved in continuous rows in relief on walls or square stelae. Beginning from around 879 BCE, these were highly detailed and were originally painted. Palace scenes depicted royal events such as Ashurbanipal's Royal Hunt of the Lion, or a war campaign, and sometimes include explanatory inscriptions. While great attention was paid to representing animals accurately and naturally, the human figures are more static and stylized.

Huge reliefs were also carved into rock faces.

A lamassu, or winged, human-headed bull.

THE ART OF WAR

As well as religious and mythological themes and scenes of nature, Mesopotamian art frequently shows the violence of war and the cruel treatment of captives, evidence of how commonplace and widespread these practices were.

A relief carving showing prisoners of war rebuilding the city of Lachish.

The Vedic people moved south into the Ganges valley and beyond. Their new territories, called the Ayarvarta after the Aryas, expanded eastwards as well, and many of the clans of the time, identified in the literature, gave their names to geographical regions that are still called by that name today. During the period in which the later Vedas were written, the Aryans covered the whole of northern India, from the Himalayas to the Vindhya mountain range in west-central India. Then, by 400 BCE, they had spread over the whole of India.

However, by the 5th century BCE, territorial identity began to replace clan identity, and eventually states were formed, struggling for supremacy and each aiming to create an empire. Kingship started to become hereditary, and the dice games, cattle raids, and chariot races, which had previously determined who would become chief, became nominal rituals. Towns were built, protected by huge ramparts of mud bricks.

At this stage kingship was thought to be divinely ordained, but was also agreed upon by common consent. Sacrifices and impressive rituals showed the power and prestige of kings, and an official hierarchy began to emerge.

Ratnins, or "jewels," assisted the king in administration. These included
- the leader of the village, who was both a civil and a military officer
- the collector of taxes
- the charioteer
- the superintendent of gambling

Modern replica of utensils and a falcon-shaped altar used for an elaborate Kuru Kingdom ritual.

- the chamberlain
- the king's hunting companion
- the courtier
- the carpenter
- the chariot maker

as well as military and religious officials such as the general and chaplain.

800–500 Later Vedic Period in India. The caste system develops, along with the concept of karma.

c.600 The Vedic religious commentaries the *Brahmanas* are codified in India.

THE CASTE SYSTEM

As Indian society became rigidly structured, the caste system developed.

- *At the top of the social pyramid was the most prestigious class, the Brahmins, the priestly caste. They held power partly because they knew how to carry out all the details of religious rituals and were able to teach the rituals. They were highly educated and learned.*
- *Below them in rank were the Kshatriyas, the nobles and soldiers who made up the fighting and ruling caste, so their duties also included administration.*
- *Next came the Vaisyas, who were farmers and traders. Both inland and overseas, trade developed, with a class of merchants called Pani. A gold bar called a riksha became a unit of value, and guilds and corporations were formed.*
- *Below the Vaisyas, at the bottom of society, came the vast mass of people who were called Shudras, and whose job was basically to serve the other three castes as laborers.*

Over time thousands of sub-castes developed depending on people's jobs, along with the Dalits, the "untouchables" who were so low in the social hierarchy that they didn't even have a caste. They would be given the worst and dirtiest jobs, and were not permitted to socialize with the other castes.

People from outside the Aryavarta, or Aryas' lands, were considered to be impure barbarians, and when they were conquered, they were automatically assigned to the lowest caste of Shudras or to the Untouchables.

A depiction of the caste system in the Vedic period, with a laborer on the left and a brahmin on the right.

THE LATER VEDIC PERIOD

THE STATUS OF WOMEN

In the Later Vedic Period women lost their privileges and neither they nor the lowest class, the Shudras, could hold property. Also, they were denied the right to perform sacrifices or read the sacred texts, and could not burn their dead. Polygamy became commonplace and the customs of dowry and child marriage developed. Daughters became undesirable.

Women lost the right to attend assemblies, and could not take part in politics. Many of the religious ceremonies formerly undertaken by the wife became the preserve of priests, and instead women were relegated to docile and subordinate domestic roles: milking cows, tending cattle, grinding corn, and carding, weaving, and dyeing wool.

However, there were some women in the academic world working as teachers and scholars, such as Gargi and Maitreyi.

At this stage the caste system was not quite as rigid as in later Indian society. There are instances of Kshatriyas becoming Brahmins due to their superior learning, for example the two Kshatriya kings Janak and Vishwamitra. There was also some rivalry between Brahmins and Kshatriyas, with each claiming superiority at times. At this time, castes could dine together and intermarry (although the higher caste would lose their status).

During the Later Vedic Period this caste system became hereditary, setting the pattern of a hierarchical Indian society for thousands of years.

Women in the Vedic Period.

98

HOLY COWS

Rice became the staple food during the Later Vedic Period, and less meat was eaten. Cows came to be considered sacred, and could not be slaughtered, though milk and milk products were popular. Agriculture was the principal occupation of the people, but peasants owning small patches of land became replaced by landlords who possessed entire villages. Elephants, oxen, and horses were used for transporting goods and to draw wagons.

Houses were made of wood and had many rooms, and along with the ever-popular pastimes of gambling and chariot racing, drama and dancing became an important part of the culture.

EDUCATION AND LEARNING

A highly developed educational system evolved during the Later Vedic Period. A special rite of passage was carried out when students were accepted by a guru or teacher, and went to live in his household or spiritual retreat. This rite still takes place in Hindu societies today on entrance to a school. Students served the guru by doing various household tasks, and in return, the guru imparted knowledge. The sacred texts the Vedas and the Upanishads, grammar, language, law, and arithmetic were all studied, and students – from all castes except the Shudras – paid a fee at the end of their studies.

An idealized depiction of a guru giving instructions to his students.

END OF AN ERA

Linguistic, cultural, and political changes marked the end of the Vedic period as a new wave of urbanization flowed though India. Indo-Greek kingdoms were established in northeastern India, parts of Afghanistan and modern Pakistan, and Hinduism and Buddhism developed.

Known as Vedism, the religion of the Vedic people is one of the traditions that shaped Hinduism. Early Vedic beliefs were also held by other Indo-European speakers, in particular the early Iranians, as can be seen by some similarities between Vedism and Zoroastrianism, such as a sacred intoxicant drink and the Upanaya, or ceremony of initiation, which involves the tying of a sacred cord by boys of the upper classes. In addition, the Vedic god Varuna corresponds to the Zoroastrian supreme deity Ahura Mazda.

However, many aspects of the *Rig Veda*, the earliest sacred text of India, are not found elsewhere and are clearly "Indian" features. It is assumed that these stem from the influence of non Indo-European indigenous peoples.

VEDIC LITERATURE

While the *Rig Veda* was composed during the Early Vedic Period up to about 800 BCE, the other three Vedas, or books of knowledge, were composed during the Later Vedic Period: the *Sama Veda*, about music and chants; the *Yajur Veda* on sacrificial ceremonies; and the *Atharva Veda*, dealing with priestly methods to ward off evil spirits and to control diseases. The *Upanishads*, the last section of the Vedas, means to sit down near a guru to learn, which was the form of education that developed during the Vedic period. Taxila, Kashi, and Ujjain were some of the important centers of learning.

During this period the Brahmanas, commentaries on the four Vedas, were also composed, along with the epic poems the *Ramayana* and the *Mahabharata*.

The *Rig Veda* is divided into ten books, each of which contains hymns, prayers, and petitions. The main ritual discussed

Pages from the *Rig Veda*.

The *Rig Veda* in Sanskrit.

c.1500–800 The *Rig Veda* is composed.

TEMPLES AND RITUALS

During the Early Vedic period, rituals were simple and were performed by householders, usually outdoors to acknowledge the power of nature. Later, the first temples were built, and religious ceremonies were carried out indoors. They became complex and elaborate rituals, involving important sacrifices, and the priestly class became devoted to finding mystic meanings in the ceremonies.

Rites of passage such as marriage or childbirth became elaborate ceremonies, and since it was customary to offer gifts to priests, such as livestock or even gold, they became wealthy and powerful.

It was believed that humans are born with debts to the gods, to ancestors, to the lower creatures and to the saints and sages. These debts are redeemed though worship, studying the Vedas, and performing certain rituals. The concept of the ascetic life also developed, as a means to attain success in life and in heaven. The ascetic retired to solitude, renouncing worldly life, and practiced celibacy and tapas – meditation with tortuous physical acts.

was the soma sacrifice, which involved taking a hallucinogenic drink which may have been made from mushrooms. There are also some references to animal sacrifice. It covers rites of marriage and death which are the same as in later Hinduism, but at this time the priests were not a hereditary class.

The Vedas were written in Sanskrit, which Hindus consider the most perfect language, and are believed to have been revealed to inspired seers. To this day the Vedas are recited in ways handed down orally from the early days of Vedic religion.

Attached to each Veda are the Brahmanas, commentaries written about 900-700 BCE and finally codified around 600 BCE. They contain explanations of rituals and myths, are particularly concerned with sacrifice, and are the oldest sources for Indian ritual.

The Aranyakas, or Forest Books, were composed around 700 BCE. They are concerned with the allegorical meaning of rituals, and were meant to be studied in a forest by students and hermits.

The Upanishads are philosophical in nature, discussing the connection between the cosmos and humanity. They are the concluding Vedic sacred texts. Composed between 700 and 500 BCE, they are concerned with the quest for supreme truth. Whereas the Brahmanas emphasize ritual, the Upanishads dwell on mystical knowledge concerning freedom from rebirth.

From the 5th century BCE onward there was a decrease in Vedic literature as writing of a more Hindu nature emerged.

KARMA

The concept of karma evolved during the Later Vedic Period. This holds that people are reborn after death and are given the opportunity to learn from previous mistakes until they live a pure life and therefore attain freedom from the cycle of rebirth. So, one's actions during life affect status and position in the next life.

GODS AND GODDESSES

The Vedas praise a wide pantheon of gods, many linked to natural phenomena, while others represent abstract qualities. Many minor deities influenced the everyday life of most people. Prajapati, or Lord of All Creatures, was the creator of the universe according to the later Vedic religion. He was said to have arisen from the primal waters, and had a female partner, known as Vac, the embodiment of the sacred, who helped create other beings. His partner is also sometimes named as Ushas, the dawn, who is also his daughter.

The gods of the *Rig Veda* were gradually demoted to become minor deities as new gods such as Vishnu, Shiva, and Rupa emerged, and the worship of Durga and Ganesh, the elephant-headed remover of obstacles, also began. The concept of a universal soul or "absolute" that dwells in everything began at this period, as did the idea of one brahman or unchanging principle. Knowledge of the relationship between atman (self) and brahman ends the cycle of birth, death, and rebirth. To know brahman is to know all.

Ganesh.

Vishnu.

Shiva.

In the second millennium BCE people speaking Indo-European languages began to migrate into Iran from Central Asia in the northeast. According to cuneiform records in Mesopotamia, by 850 BCE there were two major groups, the Medes and the Persians.

850 Mesopotamian accounts record the presence of Indo-European speakers (Aryans) in Iran. There are two major groups, Medes and Persians.

728 Median kingdom is founded by Deioces.

Cyaxares on his throne.

The Median king Cyaxares.

THE MEDIAN KINGDOM

The Medes were the first of the new Iranian Indo-European speakers to clash with Assyria. The Greek historian Herodotus reported that the Median kingdom was founded in 728 BCE by Deioces, who built the city of Ecbatana (Hamadan) as his capital. Assyrian records, however, say that at this time the Medes were merely one of several people who were becoming a nuisance on the eastern borders.

Under Cyaxares (625–585 BCE) the Medians were organized into a much more powerful army that attacked Assyria and raided the city of Assur. As a sign that they were a rising power, Babylon arranged a marriage alliance between the prince Nebuchadrezzar (later the second king of that name) and a granddaughter of Cyaxares.

In 612 the new allies turned on the terminally weak Assyrian state, and with the capture of Nineveh ended its power forever. The surviving Assyrians fled into Syria and made a fruitless appeal for help to Egypt, leaving Mesopotamia divided between Babylonia, which took the lowlands, and Media, which took the highlands.

This brought the Medes into conflict with Lydia, the dominant force in Asia Minor, but a peace treaty was arranged by the Bablyonians, and the Median kings – known as the King of Kings – were free to enjoy power over a large area of Iran and Mesopotamia for less than 100 years.

In the period between 626 and 539 BCE, Babylonia reasserted itself with the Neo-Babylonian Empire, begun by the Chaldean king Nabopolassar. Situated on the coast near the Persian Gulf, Chaldea had never been completely overthrown by the Assyrians. Becoming king in 630 BCE, in 626 Nabopolassar forced the weakening Assyrians out of Uruk, and made alliances aiming to destroy Assyria. He also fought

NEBUCHADREZZAR II (605–562 BCE)

Considered the greatest king of the Chaldean dynasty, Nebuchadrezzar (Nebuchadnezzar) II was Nabopolassar's son. He invaded and conquered Syria and Palestine, and is mainly remembered for the destruction of Jerusalem and the Babylonian Exile of the Jews.

King Nebuchadrezzar meets one of his gardeners.

Egypt, but had as many misfortunes as successes. He began to restore the network of canals around the cities of Babylonia, especially in Babylon.

c.626 The Neo-Babylonian Empire begins.

c.605–c.562 Under Nebuchadrezzar II the Chaldean Neo-Babylonian Empire becomes the most powerful state in Mesopotamia and beyond.

c.562 On the death of Nebuchadrezzar II the Neo-Babylonian Empire begins to lose power.

NEBUCHADREZZAR II'S CONSTRUCTION PROGRAM

Using the extensive wealth he obtained from conquered lands, Nebuchadrezzar began to rebuild Babylon in splendid style, transforming the city into a magnificent urban center. He rebuilt the walls, renovated the temples, including the Ezida temple and the temple to Marduk with its ziggurat, Etemenanki, and built the Processional Way paved with limestone.

Babylon is believed to have been the largest city in the world during its heyday in the 7th and 6th centuries BCE, with a population of many thousands.

The main building material was baked bricks, many of which were beautifully glazed (such as on the Gate of Ishtar), and mud bricks. The city of Babylon has now vanished apart from various remains that cover 2,100 acres (850 hectares), but it is estimated that the city originally covered twice that area.

THE ISHTAR GATE

"I placed wild bulls and ferocious dragons in the gateway and thus adorned them with luxurious splendor so the people might gaze on them in wonder," says an inscription on the Ishtar Gate attributed to Nebuchadrezzar II.

One of eight gates into the city of Babylon, this beautiful blue gate built by Nebuchadrezzar was dedicated to the goddess Ishtar. Made with glazed, cobalt-blue bricks and decorated with dragons and bulls, the Gate is now housed in the Pergamon Museum, Berlin.

Bablyon's Ishtar Gate, now in the Pergamon Museum, Berlin, Germany.

THE HANGING GARDENS OF BABYLON

One of the magnificent Seven Wonders of the World, the legendary Hanging Gardens of Babylon have, sadly, never been conclusively found – yet! The sloping walls and terraces of ziggurats were planted with trees and shrubs, probably giving rise to the image. The legend begins with King Nebuchadrezzar II, who supposedly built the gardens for his queen, Amytis, when she was homesick for the greenery and mountains of her childhood. Another legend has the Gardens in Nippur, north of Babylon, and some scholars believe the story really refers to the magnificent gardens in the Assyrian city of Nineveh, but Babylon has always been most closely associated with the Gardens.

THE DIASPORA OF THE JEWS FROM JUDAH

The first conquest of Judah by Nebuchadrezzar II took place in 598/7 BCE, and the second nearly a decade later in 587/6 BCE, with the destruction of Jerusalem and the Temple in 586 BCE. This was followed by the forced exile of large numbers of Jews to to Babylon, and the beginning of the Jewish Diaspora.

PERSIAN RULE

Cyrus the Great of Persia (born 590–580 BCE) founded the Achaemenid Persian Empire. After hearing that Nabonidus, the ruler of Babylon, and Nebuchadrezzar's last successor, was disliked not only by the people but also by the priests of Marduk, he invaded Babylon in 539 BCE and became a popular ruler. Cyrus supported local customs by giving sacrifices to local deities. As ruler of Babylonia, he inherited Palestine and Syria, and in 538 BCE, he gave the Jews permission to return to Palestine. The return happened gradually, but many Jews chose to remain in Babylon as they had become integrated into Babylonian society over the years, with some achieving high status.

Cyrus the Great.

THE DEMISE OF BABYLON

Babylonia never became independent again. In 331 BCE it passed to Alexander the Great, who wanted to make Babylon the capital of his empire, but died in Nebuchadrezzar's palace aged 32. The Seleucids, who inherited much of his territory, later abandoned it, ending one of the greatest cities in history.

Along with the ancient Egyptians, the Babylonians were one of the earliest people to use advanced math. It is possible that the Babylonians' sophisticated sciences of mathematics and astronomy were driven by their need to maintain agricultural cycles and control their systems of irrigation, so predicting celestial events and making accurate calculations were vital to society. They also needed advanced math for their administrators and traders.

Most of the early mathematics seems to have been well developed in the Old Babylonian period from about 1900 BCE.

Babylonians counted in base 60 (a sexagesimal system), whereas our modern system is decimal, base 10, which means that we only have 9 single units,

A POSITIONAL SYSTEM

Unlike the Egyptians, Babylonians used a positional or place-value notation for numbers. This uses a small number of symbols whose magnitude is determined by position. So, 72 does not mean 7 plus 2 (as it would with Egyptian or Roman numerals), but 7 times 10 plus 2. If the digits were the other way round, 27, it would be read as 2 times 10 plus 7.

They used no zero until the Seleucid period when the usage of a zero as a gap separator was introduced, but they used fractions to an extent. They could extract square roots, solve linear systems, quadratic and some cubic equations, and calculate compound interest.

Babylonians also worked with Pythagorean triples. These are three whole numbers that satisfy Pythagoras's theorem about the sides of a right-angled triangle. From the 18th century BCE Pythagoras's law was applied in Mesopotamian buildings.

ANGLES AND HOURS

The measurement of 360 that was used for the solar arc was then applied to all circles, which is why we still measure a circle in 360 degrees. For time, the day was divided into two:

12 hours for the day and 12 for the night. Each hour was divided into 60 minute – that is, tiny – sections, or minutes. In turn, they were divided into 60 even smaller "second minute" sections. So were born our hours, minutes, and seconds.

A Babylonian cuneiform tablet dealing with complicated mathematical problems, perhaps connected with architectural problems.

before we start counting larger groups of "tens," then after we reach 10 "tens" we record "hundreds," and so on. But Babylonians had 59 single units before they would measure a "sixty," and not until they reached 120 did they have another of their larger units of "sixties."

The number 60 can be divided by several numbers – 2, 3, 4, 5, 6, 10, 12, 15, 20, and 30 – so is very useful. Ten, on the other hand, can only be divided by two numbers, 2 and 5.

It is probable that the use of the base 60 system arose from the Babylonian observation that the sun took 360 days in its arc, so this measurement was divided into six equal parts.

Some cuneiform tablets are tables of values such as multiplication tables, and lists of weights and measures. These may well have been used for reference by traders or engineers. Other tablets are concerned with the solutions of algebraic or geometrical problems. Some contain up to 200 problems, of gradually increasing difficulty, and it seems likely that these were used in the demanding scribal schools. But Babylonians did not attempt to generalize their mathematics into abstract underlying theories, and not one scientific law has been found.

THE CALENDAR

During the Old Babylonian period a calendar based on the periods of the sun and the moon was in use. There were 12 months of 29 or 30 days, each beginning on the day of the first appearance of the crescent of the moon after sunset. So, the day was reckoned from sunset to sunset (still the case in Jewish and Arabic calendars). The first month was timed by the Spring Equinox or barley harvest), and an extra month was added when necessary to align with the solar year.

A Babylonian calendar listing the lucky and unlucky days of the year in cuneiform.

BABYLONIAN MATH

ASTRONOMY

Around 750 BCE important "Astronomical Diaries" were developed in which scholars looked to find the correlations between celestial phenomena and terrestrial events. They observed solstices and equinoxes, the 27-year Sirius cycle and Planetary Periods (five planets were known, as far as Saturn). In about 500–300 BCE they evolved the 19-year calendar cycle (Uruk scheme) and mapped the 360° zodiac.

Babylonian astronomy was based on meticulous observation and recording of patterns. This led to excellent celestial forecasting and a very accurate calendar, but as with their math, they did not synthesize or theorize, and had no concept of abstract space or abstract time. As far as they were concerned, their cosmology was explained in the *Enuma Elish*, a great epic poem from creation in which Marduk, the god of Babylon, placed the stars and planets in the heavens. Like humans, these were obedient to the will of Marduk and so no further explanation of their behavior was necessary.

Babylonian writings on astronomy.

The Babylonian methods and stored records became of great value to astronomers in Greece and India.

CONSTELLATIONS AND THE ZODIAC

As well as time and angular measurements, we inherited from the Babylonians many names of the stellar constellations, for example:

Modern Name	Babylonian Name
Taurus, the Bull	Steer of Heaven
Leo, the Lion	Lion
Scorpius, the Scorpion	Scorpion
Capricornus, the "Goat-Horned"	The "Goat-Fish"
Gemini, the Twins	Great Twins
Cancer, the Crab	the Crayfish

Babylonian astronomy also gave us the zodiac of 360° divided into 12 signs of 30° each, as well as the 19-year calendar cycle (used today in the Jewish and Arabic calendar, and for the timing of Easter).

كوكب راكه برفرق ودم هت سعودُ بابح كويند وكوكب شيرا بذ بابح وكوا لبُ هلا
بجوسپند كه اورا فبح كند
وان دو كوكب روشن جرم به
دنبال ستهنجسين كويند
كوكب كله الماء وهو الدلو
كواكبُ اوجبل ردو كوكب كست
ارصورت تمرخا ج ارجوش

وعربانُ كوكب شيرا كه بردوشس ركتتست مود الملك كويند وان راكه دو راكبهر
مهكيخديت يا اين كه برد بال بطورسته مودالسعود و ان برله بردوشس جنست
سببع نبو سراكه بعدا ين دوكوكبكست تهت از بود ميان سعودذبابح وان راتشبيه
كرده اند ونانبني كسود ه جيزرو مرو بردو كويند درار نو رج بارس حلم قرمو
كه يا ارصاپلو ماكاين كوكبُ طلاء بوديوان برله كه بردلدر تهتست يا املك
برس عداست مود الاجنه كويند زيراكه جون اوطلوع كند مراوم نبهان سوُ نذ
ودرز برز بمي ازمر ماكوكب شيرا ابمرخم خوست ست از جهد حنوب صفعا

الكوكب السمكين وبعا
وتانكواكب اورجنا
التا ازصورت وحبا
ناج ارصورت وان

The signs of the zodiac Capricorn and Aquarius.

111

"The wise man is one who knows what he does not know."

Laozi, *Daodejing*

The supposed founder of Daoism was the philosopher Laozi (Lao Tzi), who was thought to have lived about 604–531 BCE (practically contemporary with Confucius) in Henan province in China, and was the author of the classic book the *Daodejing* (*Tao-te-Ching*), or "The Book of the Way." Some historians now wonder if he ever actually existed or was just a *nom de plume* given by the various authors of the book.

The *Daodejing* says that although the universe appears to be complicated and bewildering, it is actually quite simple. There is one single universal principle, called the Dao or Way, which brings forth everything else in existence. Like all Daoist writings, the *Daodejing* uses metaphor, imagery, riddles, and poetry to pass on its message.

The Dao is the way of nature, the natural rhythm of the universe, a constant movement or change. It is spontaneous, free-flowing, and cyclical. But human beings spend so much time acting against nature that we have lost contact with the essential way that the world flows and the rhythm of the universe. In particular, humans try to stop change in their lives, and so lose contact with nature.

The Daoist philosopher Laozi.

Everything comes from the Dao, so everything is related, and our idea that things are separate is an illusion, which arose when we lost sight of the essential unity of the universe and began to think that our personal beliefs have an objective reality.

Daoism as a contemplative philosophy was not for everyone. It also developed into a popular communal religion with priests, ceremonies, gods, spirits, an afterlife, and moral teachings. It also degenerated into a magical cult practiced by fraudsters selling magical amulets, pretending to see

NATURE

A Daoist aims to overcome crude human nature, to harmonize with the Dao, and to become one with nature. A common way to do this is to withdraw from society, leaving earthly distractions and actions behind and seeking contemplation in nature. Even Confucian scholars, who scorned superstition, appreciated some of these aspects of Daoism.

A Daoist contemplating nature.

the future, and talking about quests for immortality or magical powers.

But it also encompassed serious searches for illumination. Skilled healers, alchemists, and martial artists were all associated with the Daoist path and concepts such as and Yin/Yang.

YIN / YANG

The way of nature expresses itself as two opposite but complementary forces, called Yin and Yang. As they constantly seek balance or harmony between themselves their interaction gives rise to movement in the universe – the seasons, the cycle of life, and so on. At their most simplistic they are described as positive and negative, or male and female, but they are much more than that. Yang is dynamic, outward-looking active energy (bright, hot, quick), while Yin is passive, inward-looking, slow, and dark. At the heart of each is the seed of the other, symbolizing the constant flow of energy between the two. The Yin/Yang balance is the basis for many traditional Chinese practises such as medicine and martial arts.

The Yin/Yang symbol. The small dots represent the seeds of the opposite energy.

ZHUANGZI AND THE BUTTERFLY

Born around 370 BCE, *Zhuangzi (Chuang Tse) was one of the great Daoist philosophers, who wrote a classic text, simply called the Zhuangzi. His writings on a dream are typical of Daoist thinking:*

> *"One night, Zhuangzi dreamed he was a butterfly – a happy butterfly, flying around and not realizing he was Zhuangzi. Suddenly he woke up, Zhuangzi again, but drowsy. And he could not tell whether he was Zhuangzi who had dreamt the butterfly or the butterfly who was dreaming it was Zhuangzi."*

A mural from a Daoist temple.

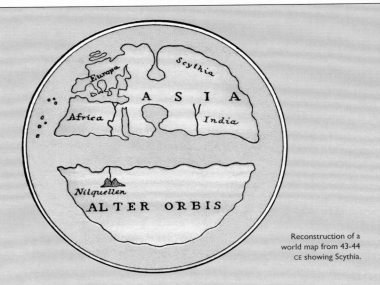

Reconstruction of a
world map from 43-44
CE showing Scythia.

Moving from southern Russia as far west as Mesopotamia, the Scythian nomads took control of western Central Asia from the 9th century until around the 4th century BCE.

Feared for their horsemanship and military skills, the Scythians grew wealthy from raiding, taking tribute from the settled farming communities on the edges of their plains, and from trading captive slaves to the Greek city-states around the Black Sea. The growth in trade eventually meant that the Scythians in the west became more settled and some intermarried with Greeks.

Scythian gold plaques, probably ornaments for clothing.

By the 4th century BCE a wealthy noble class had developed, who were buried in elaborate graves known as kurgans, often accompanied by human sacrifices. The kurgans were also filled with valuable goods such as turquoise, carnelian, and amber beads, or gold objects.

Gold-work was the major craft of the Scythians, and usually took the form of ornaments such as plaques, pectorals, necklaces, bracelets, earrings, or horse trappings, all featuring their distinctive, animal-style of decoration. Highly expressive, the animals – horses, lions, tigers, reindeer, or mythical beasts – were often shown running or fighting. As with most nomadic art, the decorated items were small and light. The many gold semi-recumbent stag figures that have been found were probably ornaments for the centers of the Scythians' round shields.

Scythian artists also used silver, bronze, iron, and electrum, and some kurgans also contained lavishly embroidered and appliquéd felt clothes, rugs, and wall hangings.

Although the Scythians were powerful enough to prevent the Persians under Darius I taking their lands in 513 BCE, by the second century BCE their culture disappeared. Scythian or Steppe art, however, lived on. It was traded by the Phoenicians around the Mediterranean and had a lasting influence on styles throughout Western Asia.

9th century The nomadic Scythians migrate west from Central Asia and form a large empire that eventually stretches from north Persia to southern Russia, and westwards to Mesopotamia and above the Black Sea.

7th century The Scythian animal-style of jewelry spreads through Western Asia.

c.513 The Scythians repel a Persian invasion.

This figured vessel shows the skill of Scythian artists.

Scythian warriors.

115

Sometime between the 7th and the 5th centuries BCE, the religion of Jainism developed in the Ganges basin of eastern India. Teaching that an ethical life will lead to freedom from repeated rebirth, Jainism emphasizes non-violence (non-injury) to all living creatures.

There was no single founding figure in Jainism, which was one of many belief systems that grew up in opposition to the Vedic Brahmanic schools of the time. These had become focused on the caste system, the declared superiority of the Brahmin priests, priestly rituals and sacrifices. In contrast, Jainism was a monastic tradition that abandoned ritual, concentrating instead on ethical living. Ascetism and non-attachment are some of the other aspects of the Jain path to spiritual purity and enlightenment.

The word Jain comes from the Sanskrit word *jina*, meaning victory, and refers to the victory of achieving spiritual illumination by one's own efforts, and thereby crossing the stream of rebirths to find salvation.

Jainism does not have a single, historical founder. Instead the tradition recognizes great teachers called Tirthankaras, literally "Ford Makers," who showed the way to cross the stream of rebirths. The first historical evidence of a

7th–5th century Jainism develops in India.

A Jain nun wears a mask to protect insects from being swallowed.

Tirthankara is of the 23rd, Parshvanatha (Parshva) in the 7th century BCE.

Jains wear veils so that they will not swallow insects or microbes, will not eat honey since they consider it the life of a bee, watch where they step so they do not crush any living thing, and avoid any jobs– like farming – where they might harm a living creature.

Twernty-four Jain Tirthankaras or spiritual teachers.

"To put the world in order, we must first put the nation in order;
to put the nation in order, we must first put the family in order;
to put the family in order, we must first cultivate our personal life ..."

Confucius, *Analects*

Confucius is the Latinized name for Kong Fuzi, or Master Kong; the true name of this philosopher was Kong Qiu. Born around 551 BCE to a poor noble family in the state of Lu in western China, he

c.141–87 Reign of Emperor Wu Di in China. He introduces the examination system for civil servants and adopts Confucianism.

died in 479 without ever knowing that he would become the most influential person in Chinese history. Only Chairman Mao had anywhere near the impact Confucius did.

During his lifetime Confucius was a fairly unimportant government official,

Confucius.

河竹后，母母上书回

丁兰，
幼年父母双
用木头刻成
商议　每日
一足禀告，
妻对木像便
指　而木像
眼中日泪

刻木事亲

Some of the teachings of Confucius on a wall.

with only a handful of dedicated students. He grew up in the tumultuous Spring and Autumn period of the Eastern Zhou dynasty, when strong central authority had broken down, and there was social chaos all round. There were no strong rulers, and very few who were moral. The historical record of the time, the *Spring and Autumn Annals*, often gloomily recorded events such as assassinations or harvests ruined by fighting.

Confucius longed for harmony, social order, and ethical behavior, virtues that he thought he recognized in a golden age of the past, during the Zhou dynasty. He was particularly struck by the story of the 11th-century Duke of Zhou, a folk hero who defended the state, acted as regent for his young nephew, and handed over the reins of power peacefully when his ward came of age.

Confucius saw this as the correct pattern of behavior, and since the ruler had behaved correctly – was benevolent, just, and ethical – the other layers of society followed suit and also behaved "properly," expressing loyalty and obedience to their superiors and behaving compassionately to their inferiors. He saw the breakdown of order and government in his own time as a breakdown of correct and ethical behavior. But he firmly believed that since people had at one time enjoyed a proper society, they could do so again if only they lived virtuous lives.

Although he envisaged the perfect society as strictly hierarchical, it was based on benevolent relationships between the superior and the inferior, and, through education, everyone could gain a better status in society. Confucius thought that human hierarchies or social orders mirrored the order of heaven, an impersonal force whose pattern was approached through the rituals of the time, especially those to do with heaven or ancestor worship. Therefore he believed that rituals should be acted out meticulously, and the inner virtue gained from following the rules correctly could help transform one into a better person all round. Better individuals led to a better society, he taught.

He was anxious that ritual should not be empty of meaning. "If you do not know how to serve the living, how do you know how to serve the dead?" he asked.

The main Confucian values were compassion, righteousness, justice, propriety, loyalty, filial piety, and honesty.

Although Confucius was unable to convince any of the rulers of his time to adopt his principles, his teachings did attract a small but dedicated band of followers. After his death they gathered together his sayings into one of the classic Chinese texts, the Analects of Confucius, and kept his ideas alive.

One of his ideals was the "Golden Rule" – don't do to other people that which you would not like them to do to you.

THE CONFUCIAN FAMILY

Confucianism regarded human social institutions such as family, school, community, and the state as essential to human flourishing and moral excellence. In particular, he thought that the family was the perfect microcosm for expressing virtuous thought and behavior. It involved all his preoccupations:
- love and loyalty
- a natural order and a proper hierarchy (with, as was natural for the times, a male figure in charge)
- filial respect

- education and learning
- a range of natural relationships, whether parent to child, older sibling to younger, child to grandparent
- morality and ethical behavior
- reverence for the shared past

He laid the groundwork for a concept that has lasted in China until today: nothing is stronger than family. His respect for ancestors and tradition deepened the cult of ancestor veneration that was already strong in China.

A STATE IDEOLOGY

When the first Han emperor established his dynasty in 206 BCE, he rejected the Qin philosophy of rule by brutality. Instead he turned to Confucius's theory that rule by virtue would unify all sections of society. Though the great sage was not there to see it, his ideas were adopted as official state ideology, and would remain the backbone of Chinese culture until the 20th century CE. Even more, since China had a huge influence on Asian nations, Confucianism had a major part to play in countries as varied as Japan and Vietnam. Overall, Confucianism has been followed by more people than any other ideology in the world.

Confucius depicted holding one of his *Analects* in a library.

CONFUCIAN SCHOLAR- OFFICIALS

When the Han emperors adopted Confucian ideas for their social structure and government, they began a system that lasted even when ruling dynasties died. All government officials had to pass examinations in Confucian theory, learn the Confucian Classics by heart, and express their understanding in artistic ways.

The Confucian Classics included his *Analects*, three other books on human wisdom, and the Five Classics of Chinese literature such as the *Yi Jing* (*I Ching*) or "Classic of Change" – a manual of divination – along with the historical record the *Annals of Spring and Autumn*.

Some commentators think that Confucianism put too much emphasis on the rightfulness of social hierarchies, but records show that at one point (much later on, during the Ming dynasty that began in the 14th century CE), nearly half the successful Confucian officials came from families with no previous connections to the bureaucracy. Confucius believed that virtue was its own reward.

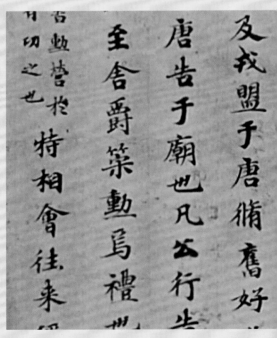

MENCIUS

The most influential Confucianist philosoper after Confucius himself, Mencius (Mengzi or Master Meng), lived from about 372 to 289 BCE. His theory of moral psychology proposed that goodness can be cultivated through discipline and education, or can be dissipated through negative behavior.

The influential Confucian philosopher Mencius.

The Chinese Spring and Autumn Annals.

It is thought that caves were first dug into the soft volcanic rock of Turkey's Cappadocia region in the 8th century BCE. Over the centuries the caves became caverns, which became whole cities, with several levels of occupation and miles of tunnels.

8th century people living in Cappadocia, Asia Minor, begin to carve out caves in the soft volcanic rock. Over time huge underground cities are created.

5th century CE, Derinkuyu is completed and is connected to the nearby city of Kaymakli by a 5-mile-long (8 km) tunnel.

16th-century map of Anatolia from Münster's *Cosmographia* showing Capadocia.

The city at Derinkuyu reached 200 feet (60 m) underground and could house 20,000 people and their livestock. With massive stone doors, it could be completely closed off, and the inhabitants could survive sieges by the use of deep wells.

Derinkuyu was completed by the 5th century CE, and was connected to the nearby city of Kaymakli by a 5-mile-long (8 km) tunnel.

Around the beginning of the first millennium CE Cappadocia was one of several regions in Asia Minor, aong with Cilicia, Pontus, and Galatea. Earlier Anatolian kingdoms had included Phrygia, one of whose kings, Midas, was said to have had the golden touch. Another Phrygian king, Gordius, created the complicated Gordian knot that no one could unravel until Alexander the Great. The soldier-king simply drew his sword and slashed the Gordian Knot apart.

The underground city of Derinkuyu in Cappadocia.

Known as Achaemenids or Achaemenians after the legendary founder of their dynasty, Achaemenes, the people who had settled in the Fars region of Iran were only loosely part of the Median confederation. In 550 BCE the Achaemenian king Cyrus II, having built up support from other groups in Iran, rebelled against the Medes and seized control of the Median kingdom. His descendants would go on to form the largest empire the world had then seen.

CYRUS THE GREAT

Cyrus II, the founder of the first Persian Empire, earned the title Cyrus the Great not just for his military victories, but also for his diplomacy and humane treatment of conquered people.

As with so many great figures of history, Cyrus's childhood attracted folk stories and legends, recorded by the Greek historian Herodotus. We do not know when or where Cyrus was born, but it was probably in the Fars region of Persia between 590 and 580 BCE. "Cyrus" may

c.549 Cyrus the Great conquers the Medes and founds the Achaemenid Persian Empire.

c.539 Babylon falls to Cyrus of Persia.

c.538 Cyrus the Great allows the Jewish exiles to return to Judah. The Jews return and build the second Temple in Jerusalem.

c.529 Death of Cyrus the Great, succeeded by Cambyses.

c.521 Darius the Great takes over the Persian Empire.

c.518 Darius the Great founds the city of Persepolis.

6th century The traditional date for the life of the Persian prophet Zoroaster (Zarathustra).

By 486 Darius the Great of Persia has the Behistun Inscription carved into a cliff in western Iran.

c.485 Xerxes I becomes Persian Emperor.

c.480 The Persians under Xerxes invade Greece. Persia defeats Sparta at the Battle of Thermopylae, and is defeated at the naval Battle of Salamis.

c.465 Death of Xerxes I of Persia.

c.401 Battle of Cunaxa near Babylon. The rebellious Cyrus the Younger is defeated by Artaxerxes II of Persia. The "Retreat of the Ten Thousand" as 10,000 of Cyrus's Greek mercenaries, under Xenophon, fight their way north to safety.

The Achaemenid Empire.

Cyrus the Great, King of Persia.

in fact have been a title or throne name rather than his personal name, because after the fall of the Persian Empire it does not seem to have been used.

Cyrus was the son of Cambyses I of Persia and a daughter of the Median king Astyages, who was then the Persian overlord. According to legend, Astyages had a dream that the baby would be a threat to him, so he ordered that Cyrus should be killed. As in all such stories, the official entrusted with killing the child could not carry through with the deed, so instead gave the baby to a shepherd family to look after. The boy showed such amazing abilities and strength of character that he came to the attention of Astyages, who mellowed and allowed Cyrus to live.

The dream was true, though. As a grown man, Cyrus turned on his grandfather and took the kingdom from him.

By the standards of the time, Cyrus was incredibly humane. He did not massacre the inhabitants of conquered cities, and he even spared the kings he fought against, such as Croesus of Lydia. He won support from conquered peoples by allowing them to continue their religious practices as well as many local customs of government. He insisted that everyone in his empire should have the same rights under the law. When the Jewish people who had been held captive in Babylon asked to be allowed to return to Judea, Cyrus not only agreed to their petition, but he restored to them some of the Temple treasures that Nebuchadrezzar of Babylon had taken.

One of Cyrus's records says: "It is the law, henceforth, that the strong shall not injure the weak. I, Cyrus ... enforce the law."

Previous conquerors of Mesopotamian cities had often committed atrocities, and a popular way of expressing superiority had been to tear down temples and palaces. So when Cyrus entered the captured city of Babylon in 529 BCE, it is reported that the priests stood by, expecting him to order the destruction of their temples and statues, and instead, when Cyrus laid his rod of office at the feet of the statue of Marduk, Babylon's most important deity, the high priest broke down in tears. He picked up Cyrus's rod, returned it to the king, and declared him to be the rightful ruler of the city.

Cyrus's records say about his entry into Babylon: "I assumed the throne of

the king. My great army entered the city without incident. I accorded to all men the freedom to worship their own gods ... I ordered that no house be destroyed, that no inhabitant be dispossessed. I gave peace and quiet to all men."

By giving freedom of worship, by freeing people from local tyrants, by ruling with tolerance, and by imposing

- **c.336** Darius III, the last Persian Achaemenid emperor, ascends to the throne.
- **c.333** Battle of the Issus: Alexander the Great defeats Darius III of Persia.
- **c.331** Scythians repel and kill Alexander the Great's viceroy.
- **c.330** Battle of Gaugemela: Alexander the Great's final victory over Darius III of Persia. Alexander becomes ruler of the Persian Empire.

AS RICH AS CROESUS

Croesus was the last king of Lydia, a commercial state in western Anatolia with its capital at Sardis. It is thought that the Lydians invented metal coins (gold and silver), and also introduced the first permanent shops. The kingdom reached its height around 600 BCE, but was absorbed by the Persian Empire in 546 BCE.

Croesus extended the kingdom by conquest, and was fabulously wealthy, giving rise to the saying "As rich as Croesus." He was particularly noted for giving extravagant donations to the Oracle at Delphi. The Lydians had a major influence on the commercial development of their Ionian Greek neighbors.

Croesus, King of Lydia, brought before Cyrus the Great of Persia.

There are different accounts of what happened to Croesus. Some say he died in his burning citadel under Persian attack, others say that he became an advisor to his conqueror, Cyrus the Great of Persia.

CAMPAIGNS OF CYRUS THE GREAT

550 Iran
Cyrus cemented his rule over the east of Persia (Iran) before turning his attention to the Medes in the west. He defeated his grandfather Astyages, the last Median king, when large numbers of Median troops deserted to join the new rising star.

547–46 Lydia
Cyrus first looked north, to wealthy Lydia in Asia Minor. He occupied Cilicia, isolating Lydia from any potential help from other powers such as Egypt or Babylon. Late in 547 BCE the Persians and Lydians fought an inconclusive battle on the Halys River, and thinking that the battle season was over for the year, the Lydians disbanded and returned to their capital of Sardis. However Cyrus did not, in turn, return home. Instead, he pressed on, besieged Sardis, and captured the Lydian king Croesus in 546.

545 Central Asia
Cyrus subdued tribes to the east of Persia in Afghanistan and Pakistan, and beyond the Oxus River.

Before 540 West Asia Minor
Cyrus's generals accepted the surrender of Miletus and conquered the other Greek city-states on the western coast of Asia Minor.

539 Babylon
With an unpopular king, Nabonidus, in Bablyon, there was internal dissent that Cyrus took full advantage of, entering the city after barely a struggle. When he showed that he would rule not as a foreign conqueror but as a Babylonian, he was accepted as a legitimate king. The Babylonian territories he then absorbed into the empire stretched to the borders of Egypt, and included Judea.

529 Eastern Frontier
Cyrus was preparing to attack Egypt when he was called to the east to defend the borders. He died fighting near the Oxus and Jaxartes rivers.

    Cyrus the Great was succeeded by his son Cambyses, who attacked Egypt, leaving garrisons there when he hastened back to Persia in 522 to crush an imposter. He died from infection that year, leaving a potentially disastrous power vacuum.

human rights for all, Cyrus won the loyalty of his people and the respect of his enemies. The Greek philosopher Plato wrote that Cyrus encouraged people to offer him advice, and therefore profited from the experience and intelligence of advisers throughout the empire, and that "harmony prevailed throughout the country." Plato went on: "Cyrus was a great leader and a great friend of his people. He gave to all of them the rights of free men. And by that he won their hearts

The state entry of Cyrus into Babylon..

and his soldiers stood ready to face any peril."

Cyrus set the standard for the Persian Empire by frowning on slavery, athough it undoubtedly did occur, especially the sale of prisoners of war.

The Greek writer Xenophon chose Cyrus as his model of what a great military commander should be, and also a great ruler. To his own people, Cyrus was known as the "father of the people," who it would appear held him in affection.

127

THE BATTLE OF MARATHON: THE GRECO–PERSIAN WARS BEGIN

Darius saw his actions against Greece as an act of vengeance. In 492 BCE he launched a naval expedition, which was forced to withdraw by storms. Two years later, a new Persian invasion force set out with the intention of subduing the Athenians and launching a conquest of mainland Greece.

Commanded by the general Datis, the Persian force numbered between 15,000 and 20,000, and included their lethal cavalry troops. Under the overall command of the Athenian Militiades, some 10,000 Athenians and 1,000 of their Plataean allies marched to the plains of Marathon to meet the invaders. Athens had sent to the other major Greek state, Sparta, for help, but the Spartans gave the excuse that they were taking part in an important religious festival, so could not send any soldiers.

The invasion force landed in the bay before Marathon in September 490, but the Greeks had already chosen the battleground, using marshes and mountainous terrain so that the Persian cavalry could not be deployed.

Militiades reinforced the Greek flanks, so when he launched a frontal attack, the Persians were lured into the centre, then simply overwhelmed as the Greek flanks attacked from the sides. The Persians fled back to their ships, but were slaughtered as they retreated. About 6,400 Persians were killed, while the Athenians claimed a loss of only 192 (and an unknown number of Plataeans).

Marathon was one of history's decisive battles. In the first place it was a shock defeat for an army that had previously been thought to be invincible. Secondly, it showed how well the disciplined Greek infantry could perform, and in the third place it encouraged the other Greek states to resist the Persian Empire.

Infuriated, Darius prepared an even stronger invasion force, but was diverted by a rebellion in Egypt in 486 BCE. He died later that year, leaving his son, Khshayarsha, who is better known by his Greek name of Xerxes, on the throne. In the Bible, Xerxes was called Ahasuerus.

The Battle of Marathon between the Persians and the Greeks in 490 BCE.

DARIUS THE GREAT

Darius I, the Great, one of Cyrus's generals and a cousin of his, seized the throne in 521 BCE and crushed rebellions in Persia. To reduce the possibility of future unrest, he continued Cyrus's plan to reorganize the empire into satrapies (districts), each with a satrap or governor.

Darius extended the empire to northwest India, strengthened its eastern borders, and then attempted to crush the Scythians north of the Bosphorus River. This was the first Persian incursion into Europe, and although he failed to engage the Scythians in a decisive battle, he did lay claim to Thrace and Macedonia.

In a surprise move, the Greek city-states in Ionian Asia Minor launched a concerted rebellion in 500 BCE, burning Sardis, the city of the local satrap, in 498. Athens provided some military support to the Ionians, a move that brought them the lasting enmity of the Persians. It was not until 494 that Persia began to regain the rebellious cities.

DARIUS'S TRANSLATIONS

The main record of Darius's early years as Persian emperor provided an invaluable opportunity to translate ancient cuneiform scripts. He had inscriptions relating the events leading to his ascension as emperor carved into rocks, the most important being the trilingual rock relief on a cliff at Mount Behistun in Kermanshah, Iran.

Darius the Great with attendants.

129

Darius the Great of Persia conquering rebels.

The Athenian general Miltiades (550-489 BCE) played an important role in the Battle of Marathon.

Inscribed in three different cuneiform scripts of the same text, Old Persian, Elamite, and Babylonian Akkadian, the Behistun Rock allowed scholars to cross-translate from Persian and so decipher the previously mysterious cuneiform scripts of Babylonian and Elamite. It is the Persian and Babylonian equivalent of the Egyptian Rosetta Stone.

The Behistun Rock is on an ancient road running between Babylon and Ecbatana, the capital cities of Babylonia and Media. The inscription itself is a massive 49 feet (15 m) high and 82 feet (25 m) wide, and was carved at a height of 328 feet (100 m) up the cliff.

Darius was a great builder, bringing craftsmen and raw materials from all over the empire. He built a whole new city at Persepolis in Persis (Fars) to act as a second capital, and added a new palace and audience hall in Susa, the first capital. He also authorized new temples in Egypt

Trilingual relief of Darius, Bisitun, Iran

and approved the rebuilding of the Jewish Temple in Jerusalem.

Describing the materials for his new palace in Susa, Darius recorded cedar from Lebanon, gold from Sardis and Bactria, lapis-lazuli and carnelian from Sogdiana, turquoise from Chorasmia, silver and ebony from Egypt, ornamentation from Ioniam and ivory from Ethiopia. He wrote:

"The stone-cutters who wrought the stone, those were Ionians and Sardians. The goldsmiths ... were Medes and Egyptians. The men who wrought the wood, those were

Persepolis, the ceremonial capital of the Achaemenid Empire.

A ruined palace in Persepolis, Iran.

XERXES

Starting his reign as Persian Emperor with a rebellion in Egypt and facing an uprising in Babylon about 482 BCE, Xerxes was a much harsher ruler than his predecessors. He suppressed the rebellions quickly and firmly, then imposed Persian rules instead of allowing the local customs to continue. After he failed to crush the Greeks, Xerxes spent more and more time in his luxurious palaces, setting the stage for the later decadence that characterized the end of the Persian Empire. He allowed harem intrigues and plots to weaken the empire, and was assassinated in 465 BCE. There was only one strong Persian emperor after Xerxes, and the Empire was completely unprepared to face the might of Alexander the Great less than 100 years later.

Emperor Xerxes I of Persia.

A glazed brick frieze from the Achaemenid palace in Susa showing soldiers of the Persian army.

Sardians and Egyptians. The men who wrought the baked brick, those were Babylonians. The men who adorned the wall, those were Medes and Egyptians."

The Persians themselves were particularly skilled at decorative arts, such as goldwork and jewelry, seal cutting, pottery, and fine metalwork such as decorated weapons.

THE GRECO–PERSIAN WARS CONTINUE

The sea battle of Salamis between the Persians and the Greeks in 480 BCE.

In 481 BCE, Xerxes took his land and sea forces north to invade Greece again. After spending the winter in Sardis in Asia Minor, the invasion force met a Greek force at the narrow mountain pass of Thermopylae on the northern shore of the Gulf of Lamia, east-central Greece.

Leonidas, King of Sparta, commanded about 7,000 Greeks as well as his own band of 300 Spartans. Vastly outnumbered, his aim was to buy time for the Greeks to withdraw to a defensive line at the Corinth isthmus and gather allies. Led by the general Mardonius, the Persians found a mountain path that enabled them to take the Greeks by surprise, and in a heroic last stand, the Spartans fought to the death to give the main troops time to withdraw.

The Battle of Thermopylae became a symbol of heroic resistance, but despite their sacrifice the Spartans were unable to stop the Persians pressing on to Athens and burning down the Acropolis. The turning point came at the naval Battle of Salamis, when the Persian fleet was driven out of Greek waters. The first decisive naval battle in history, the battle saw the Persians lose up to 300 galleys out of their fleet of 600, while the Greeks lost 40 out of 366 triremes.

Salamis delayed further attacks by the Persian army, but the real end of the invasion was the Battle of Plataea in 479 BCE, when an alliance of Greek troops decisively defeated the Persians, killing the general Mardonius. It was the end of the Greco–Persian Wars, though from then on Persia often used its wealth to try and influence Greek affairs.

ACHAEMENIAN ADMINISTRATION

The Persian emperors used the title "King of Kings," implying that they were at the top of a social pyramid that also included lesser kings. But as with Persian art and architecture, social systems were adopted from all around the empire. These lesser kings may have formed part of the emperor's court, moving with him from city to city.

Darius the Great's administrative reforms, begun by Cyrus the Great, introduced a system of satrapies or districts, governed by a satrap. In each satrapy an army was stationed, led by a general reporting directly to the emperor, as well as an administrative official to collect taxes. Keeping these potentially powerful men under control was a roaming band of inspectors, known as the "king's eyes," and the local officials would often also be moved to a different district to prevent the build-up of a local power base.

The work of the "king's eyes" was helped by a government postal system and the construction of a road network with relay stations a day's ride apart from each other. Together with the construction of a canal between the Nile and the Red Sea (an early Suez Canal), this gave the Persians better communications than any previous state in the region. Coins, weights, and measures were standardized, and Darius was particularly proud of the legal system he founded. This involved local courts based on local custom, and imperial laws issued by the king. He wrote: "Much that was ill-done, I made good. My law of that they feel fear, so that the stronger does not smite nor destroy the weak."

Darius replaced the military levy with a standing army, including an elite 10,000 "immortals" from whom the personal royal guard was chosen. At times of war the army was reinforced by a military levy, but overall, Darius made his mark as an administrator, not a soldier, on an empire that managed to allow a huge range of people, each with their own customs and religions, to thrive under the centralized authority of one King of Kings.

The god Ahura Mazda with King Ardashir I, the founder of the Persian Sasanian Empire.

ZARATHUSTRA AND ZOROASTRIANISM

It was probably under Darius the Great that Zoroastrianism became the state religion of Persia. He himself was definitely a follower: on the Behistun Rock Darius attributes his success to "the grace of Ahura Mazda," the Zoroastrian god. This is the first written mention of Ahura Mazda.

The religion rose from the prophet and teacher Zarathustra, known as Zoroaster in Greek, who probably lived in the northeast of the Iranian plateau sometime between 1,000 and 600 BCE. The region has stark contrasts of desert and fertile land, mountains and plains, heat and cold, and as Zarathustra traveled with the semi-nomadic peoples of the region, he came to see that humanity was also dominated by contrasting forces.

Zarathustra viewed the spiritual world in similar dualistic terms. To him, the creator god Ahura Mazda – god of light and life, and creator of everything pure – was locked in a struggle with the destructive Ahriman, who represented evil, death, and darkness. Humanity was trapped in the middle of this battle, but was given free will by Ahura Mazda, so could make a conscious choice of good or evil.

Emphasizing the need for ethical behavior and truth, Zarathustra said that human beings have within us the ability to resist evil and to turn to Ahura Mazda. He opposed previous religious practises such as animal sacrifice and the use of hallucinogenic plants, and made fire, as a symbol of truth, the center of ritual. He clashed with the magi, the traditional priest class of the Medes and Persians, but also won the patronage of some chiefs.

Zoroastrianism became the state religion of Persia, probably under Darius the Great.

Winged symbol of Ahura Mazda, worshipped by the Zoroastrians. Persepolis: Royal Audience Hall of Darius.

Zarathustra.

Although Hinduism may possibly be the world's oldest religion, with its roots more than 5,000 years ago in Vedic India and other traditions, its modern form did not evolve until around 500 to 300 BCE. There was no one single founder of the religion or any one single holy text; instead Hinduism encompasses a broad range of philosophies and literature, connected by rituals, concepts, sacred sites, and practices. Its scriptures include the Vedas, the Upanishads, the *Bhagavad Gita* and the Agamas, and the main connecting thread is the desire to achieve moksha or salvation/liberation. The word "Hindu" comes from a Persian word meaning people of the Indus Valley.

Hindus consider that human life has four aims:

- dharma (ethics/duties)
- artha (prosperity/work)
- kama (passions/desires)
- moksha (salvation/liberation).

The two most important goals for human beings are dharma, in order to sustain harmony and order, and moksha, the release from the cycle of rebirth. In the epic

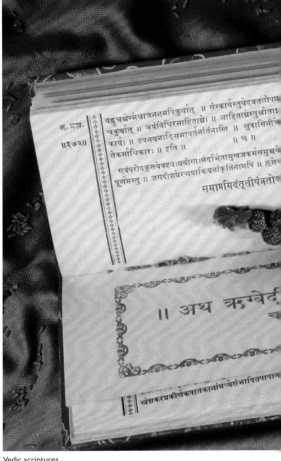

Vedic scriptures.

HINDU DEITIES

The Hindu concept of God is complex since the religion contains pantheistic thought (equating god with the universe), polytheistic and monotheistic ideas, and even atheism: different schools of Hinduism argue variously for a creator god, a non-creator god, or are non-theistic. Some sects see Brahman as the Supreme Being and worship aspects of this supreme god such as Brahma the creator of the universe, Vishnu the preserver, and Shiva the destroyer. Rama and Krishna, the heroes of the epic poems the *Ramayana* and the *Mahabharata*, were incarnations of Vishnu.

The divine can be found in humans, animals, trees, and rivers, and from ancient times there was a strong tradition

c.500–300 Hinduism evolves into its modern form.

c.300 Indian traders spread Hinduism to Indonesia.

c.100 Indian traders found a kingdom in Malaysia. Hinduism and Buddhism spread through the peninsula.

c.250–500 CE The *Puranas*, Hindu religious texts, are composed.

poem the *Mahabharata*, the god Krishna defines dharma as preserving the affairs of both the material and the celestial worlds. As far as moksha is concerned, in some schools of thought release from rebirth can only occur in the after-life, whereas other schools consider it attainable in this life through the realization of one's eternal relationship with god liberating the self from continual suffering in this world.

Other important Hindu themes include karma (action and consequence), and various yogas (paths). Karma explains that the present circumstances of life are consequences of past actions, and also that actions today will affect future lives. The worship of deities, recitations, meditation, rites of passage, festivals, and pilgrimage are all practiced. Eternal duties include honesty, patience, compassion, self-restraint, and not harming other living beings.

of the divine feminine. Goddesses such as Lakshmi, the goddess of good fortune, Durga, the goddess of moral order, and Kali, the destroyer of evil, are just as important as gods. In addition there are celestial entities known as devas, while some traditions consider that there is a personal god or spiritual inspiration for individuals known as Ishvara.

RITUALS

Religious rituals are practiced at home, varying regionally, and are an individual choice. Typically they include lighting a lamp, offering food to idols, recitations, meditations, hymns, and chanting.

On special occasions such as weddings and funerals, the old Vedic rituals of fire oblation, and the chanting of Vedic

The Hindu holy book, the *Bhagavad Gita*, with the spiritual symbol "Om."

hymns take place. Hindus celebrate a number of sanskaras, or rites of passage: name-giving is an important sanskara, as are those concerned with pregnancy and birth. Others include the first haircut, ear-piercing, entry into school, first shave, first menses, wedding, fasting, and cremation.

PILGRIMAGES AND FESTIVALS

Many historically important pilgrimages are still undertaken, to sites such as mountains, rivers, and forests, as well as to holy men and gurus. Every year, some 40 to 100 million people undertake the mass pilgrimage to one of four river sites, including the Ganges, depending on the year. The pilgrims pray to the sun and undertake a ritual bath in the river.

Festivals link individual and social life to dharma or mark various traditional stories. Many festivals are regional, whereas others such as Holi and Diwali are pan-Hindu.

PRE-CLASSICAL HINDUISM

From around 200 BCE to 300 BCE Brahmanic thought was synthesized with Buddhist influences, Vedic religion, and even older indigenous religions. During this period the Vedas and Upanishads became central to defining Hinduism, and scholars wrote important foundational texts. Monasteries were well established by this time.

Statues of the Hindu deities Lakshmi and Narayan.

THE CLASSICAL PERIOD

The Gupta period from 320 CE is sometimes called the Hindu Classical Period. The religious texts known as the Puranas, composed between 250 and 500 CE, continued the Vedic traditions but included an expanded mythology of Hindu gods such as Vishnu, Shiva, and Devi. These texts are the beginnings of medieval Hinduism. The Gupta period saw great temples built, such as the paneled Dashavatara temple at Deogarh in Madhya Pradesh and the complex at Erakina (Eran), also in Madhya Pradesh.

Under the Guptas another tradition began, that of carving large stone statues of deities.

A temple to Vishnu in
Uttar Pradesh, India.

Considered to be one of the greatest military geniuses ever, Alexander the Great was only twenty when he inherited the throne of Macedonia in Greece as Alexander III. Within ten years he made a lasting impact on Europe, Asia, and Africa.

Born in 356 BCE in the Macedonian capital of Pella, Alexander's father was Philip II of Macedon and his mother was Olympias, the daughter of the king of Epirus. Alexander was tutored by Aristotle, one of the great Greek philosopher-scientists, giving him a breadth of vision that many contemporary rulers lacked. It is possible that Alexander not only wanted to conquer new lands, but he also simply wanted to explore them. He was also inspired by the *Iliad*, Homer's epic poem about the Trojan War, and carried with him on his conquests an annotated copy of the *Iliad* that Aristotle had given to him.

Alexander's military training started young. When his father was campaigning in Byzantium in 340, Alexander put down a revolt by the Thracian Maedi people, and at the Battle of Chaeronea against the Greek states of Athens and Thebes in 338 he was put in charge of the left wing of the army. Philip had reformed the Macedonian army, developing both the cavalry and the infantry phalanx, and for the first time since the Assyrians, used siege weapons. Victory at Chaeronea led to Philip's election as hegemon or leader of the League of Corinth, a federation of Greek states.

When Philip was assassinated at a wedding feast by his own bodyguard in 336, Alexander was proclaimed king, but quickly killed his cousin and other people

Alexander the Great founding the city of Alexandria.

who might have a claim on the throne. He had to quell several revolts, but he too was given the title of hegemon and put in command of the planned Greek invasion of Persia.

PERSEPOLIS BURNS

Most Persian cities pragmatically opened their gates to the new ruler, and Alexander visited Babylon and Susa peacefully. The satrap of Persepolis however, attempted to defend the city and Alexander was forced to fight. In revenge, he allowed his troops to loot the city. A fire broke out in the palace, burning it down and spreading around the city. There are different accounts of how this happened: it was possibly deliberate retribution for the burning of Athens during the Greco–Persian Wars, or it may have been the result of a drunken accident. Alexander was well known for his liking for alcohol.

336 Alexander the Great becomes king of Macedonia.

c.334 Alexander the Great invades Persia through Anatolia, winning the Battle of Granicus.

333 Battle of the Issus: Alexander the Great defeats Darius III of Persia.

331 Scythians repel and kill Alexander the Great's viceroy.

330 Battle of Gaugemela: Alexander the Great's final victory over Darius III of Persia. Alexander becomes ruler of the Persian Empire.

327–6 Alexander the Great invades India.

326 Alexander the Great's last major battle, at Hydaspes in modern day Punjab. He agrees to his army's demand to return home.

323 Alexander the Great dies at Babylon.

319 Wars of the Diadochi, Alexander the Great's successors. His empire is eventually divided into three: the Macedonian, Egyptian, and Asian regions.

c.317 The last Macedonian garrisons leave India.

c.312 The Seleucid Empire is founded, controlling most of the Asian parts of Alexander the Great's empire.

c.300 The Seleucids of Persia move Greek soldiers and colonizers into Bactria in modern Afghanistan, where some of Alexander the Great's soldiers have already settled.

Following the Battle of Gaugemela, Alexander the Great comes upon the body of Darius III of Persia, and orders a proper burial for him.

THE PERSIAN CAMPAIGN

Having secured his northern border, Alexander turned towards Persia. He entered Asia Minor in 334 BCE with an army of about 30,000 infantry and more than 5,000 cavalry, and accompanied by engineers, surveyors, architects, and historians. After heavy fighting, he defeated the Persians at the Battle of the Granicus. This let him move down the Ionian coast, freeing the Greek city-states there, then proceed towards Syria. While in Asia Minor, Alexander made a point of visiting the site of Troy and the grave of Achilles, his great hero.

In 333 Alexander and the Persian King Darius III met at the Battle of the Issus in Syria, where the Greeks defeated

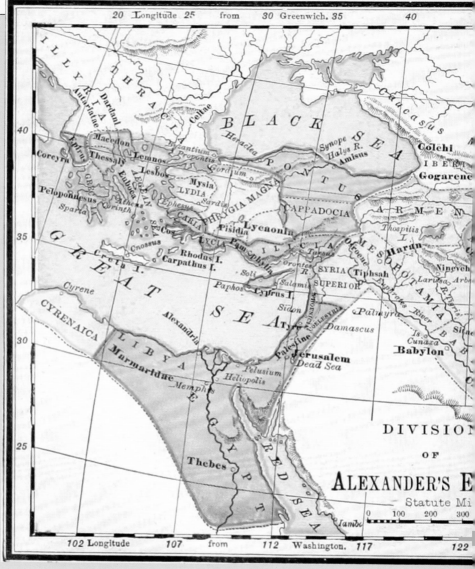

Map of the division of Alexander's Empire.

the numerically superior Persian forces. Darius fled, but his wife, mother, and two daughters were captured. When Darius offered a ransom and territorial concessions for their freedom, Alexander replied that since he himself was now king of Asia, he was the one who would decide any territorial divisions.

After Syria, most of the Levant fell to the Greeks, followed by Egypt, and in 331 BCE Alexander turned back towards Mesopotamia. For the second and final time he met Darius III in battle at Gaugamela, and once again forced the Persian king to flee. Darius had summoned the might of his empire: fifteen war elephants from India and

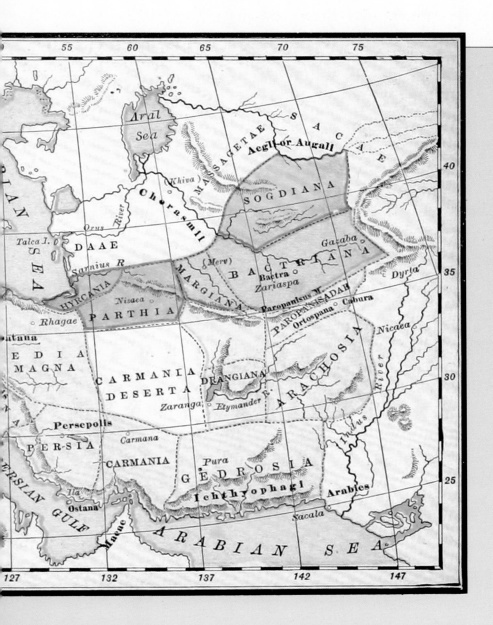

an army of a reported million men. But the elephants proved ineffective against the well-trained Greeks, and the Persian's fearsome scythe-bearing chariots failed to cause chaos in the Greek ranks since the phalanxes simply moved aside to avoid them.

Darius fled east hoping to raise another army, but the last Persian emperor was killed by one of his own satraps, Bessus, and left lying in a cart beside the road. Alexander was furious to see a king treated like this, and later had Bessus executed. Aged just 25, Alexander was now ruler of the vast Persian Empire as well as Macedonia.

Alexander wanted still more. He led his often reluctant troops onwards a further 11,000 miles to the east, subduing clans and kingdoms as he went, and in 327 BCE crossed the Hindu Kush mountain range near the Afghan-Pakistan border. The following year he won a costly victory against Porus, King of the Pauravas, at Hydaspes in modern-day Punjab, but his men had had enough. When they demanded they should return to Macedonia, Alexander reluctantly agreed, appointing Porus as the local satrap and leaving just a few garrisons on this most easterly point of his empire.

DEATH OF A LEGEND

A legend in his own lifetime, Alexander never lost a battle. He was a great military strategist, kept the loyalty of his troops, was prepared to take risks (often foolhardy ones), and was also extremely lucky in battle. Adding territory to the Persian lands he conquered, his empire stretched from Greece to the Indian Punjab, and from the Danube to Egypt. He founded a great many towns (usually named Alexandria or some other variation of his own name), introduced a common Greek culture and language, and insisted that everyone in his empire

The death of Alexander the Great at Babylon in 323 BCE.

THE DIADOCHI

Asked on his deathbed to name his successor, Alexander replied "The strongest." Since he had no clear-cut heir, he knew there would be a power struggle after his death, and only the strongest would emerge alive, let alone in a position of power.

Greek for "successors," the Diadochi is the name given to Alexander's generals and friends who, just as he had anticipated, fought among themselves for control of his empire.

At first the succession was civilized. The generals agreed that the empire should be shared jointly by Alexander's half-brother Arrhidaeus and his unborn child should it be a boy, which it was, becoming Alexander IV of Macedonia. The generals each took a satrapy to govern, but it was not long before the Wars of the Diadochi broke out in 319 BCE.

By 310 both the nominal kings had been murdered, the provinces of the empire had become independent, and the surviving generals had taken the title of kings, but it was another 30 years before the conflict ended and Alexander's empire was effectively divided into three. The Antigonids, descendants of Antigonus, took Macedonia; the Ptolemies, descendants of Ptolemy, took Egypt; and the Seleucids, descendants of Seleucus, controlled Asia.

The Wars of the Diadochi.

should be treated equally, except for himself. He attempted to introduce the Persian ceremonial custom of prostration, although his Macedonians simply laughed at the idea, and toward the end of his life he declared that he should be treated as if he were divine.

Alexander could be brutal and vengeful. When a group of Greek mercenaries fighting for Persia tried to surrender at the Battle of Granicus, he ordered that they should be killed. And if he was badly wounded in battle or faced particularly stubborn opposition he often reacted by killing all the enemy men and selling the women and children into slavery.

To try and unite the Macedonians and Persians, Alexander arranged for himself and 80 of his officers to marry Persian women in a mass ceremony. Practically none of the marriages lasted. Alexander had already married Roxana, the daughter of a Central Asian chieftain, in order to cement an alliance. When he died suddenly in Babylon in 323 at the age of 33 (possibly because of a prolonged bout of drinking), Roxana was pregnant with his posthumous son.

INDIA'S LARGEST EMPIRE

The largest empire in Indian history, the Mauryan Empire lasted from 321 to 185 BCE. Founded by Chandragupta Maurya, it eventually encompassed the whole of the subcontinent except the Tamil south and was one of the most populous empires of the ancient world, with a population of 50–60 million. It was a highly developed autocracy with a standing army and a civil service. With its capital at Pataliputra (Patra) near the Ganges river, under the Mauryas trade, economic activity, and agriculture all flourished.

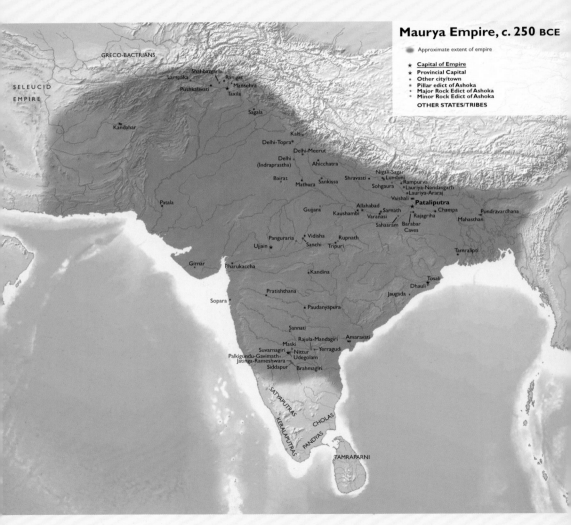

Maurya Empire, c. 250 BCE

Approximate extent of empire

★ Capital of Empire
★ Provincial Capital
• Other city/town
• Pillar edict of Ashoka
• Major Rock Edict of Ashoka
• Minor Rock Edict of Ashoka
OTHER STATES/TRIBES

GRECO-BACTRIANS

SELEUCID EMPIRE

Lampaka
Shahbazgarhi
Ramgat
Pushkalavati
Mansehra
Taxila

Kandahar

Sagala

Kalsi
Delhi-Topra
Delhi-Meerut
Delhi (Indraprastha)
Ahicchatra
Bairat
Mathura
Sankissa
Shravasti
Nigali-Sagar
Lumbini
Rampurva
Sohgaura
Lauriya-Nandangarh
Lauriya-Araraj
Vaishali

Patala

Gujjara
Allahabad
Kaushambi
Sarnath
Varanasi
Champa
Pataliputra
Pundravardhana
Rajagriha
Sahasram
Barabar Caves
Mahasthan

Panguraria
Vidisha
Rupnath
Ujjain
Sanchi
Tripuri

Girnar
Bharukaccha
Kandina
Tamralipti

Pratishthana
Dhauli
Tosali
Jaugada

Sopara
Paudanyapura

Sannati
Rajula-Mandagiri
Amaravati
Maski
Suvarnagiri
Yerragudi
Palkigundu-Gavimath
Nittur
Jatinga-Rameshwara
Udegolam
Siddapur
Brahmagiri

SATYAPUTRAS
KERALAPUTRAS
CHOLAS
PANDYAS

TAMRAPARNI

c.320 Chandragupta Maurya founds the Mauryan dynasty in India.

305 After defeating the forces of Seleucus I Nicator, the Mauryan Empire in northern India takes parts of southern Afghanistan, introducing Buddhism to the region.

c.300 Nomadic Parthians move into West Asia from the north.

c.300 The local folk religions of Japan begin to syncretize into Shinto.

270 After a power struggle, Ashoka becomes the Mauryan emperor in India.

262 The Kalinga Wars in India end with the Mauryans in control of most of the country.

185 The Shungas replace the Mauryan dynasty in India.

THE LEGEND OF CHANDRAGUPTA MAURYA

Chandragupta Maurya was born around 340 BCE. He was raised by a cowherd after his father, a chief, was killed in a border skirmish. Later, he was sold as a slave, and was bought by the politician Kantilya, who took him to Taxila (now in Pakistan), where he was educated. He is said to have dreamt that he was licked by a lion and met Alexander the Great, prompting him to believe in his future royalty.

Advised by Kantilya, Chandragupta gathered mercenaries from many regions and around 325 BCE he took the throne of the Magadha kingdom (Bihar) in northwest India. Following the death of Alexander the Great in 323, Chandragupta was able to conquer the Punjab, ending the Nandra dynasty there. The Macedonian garrisons left on Alexander's borders may have supported him against the Nandra. Chandragupta's army was also made up of a wide range of soldiers including Himalayans, Persians, Bactrians, and Scythians. In 305 he fought the Greek inheritor of Alexander the Great's eastern lands, Seleucus I Nicator, and established his border with Persia. Chandragupta and Seleucus signed a peace treaty in 303, with a marital alliance.

Seleucus received 500 war elephants, while Chandragupta received the eastern satrapies of the Seleucid Empire, including Kandahar and Baluchistan. Subsequently, several Greeks were at the Mauryan court, including the diplomats Megasthenes and Dionysius.

Chandragupta is thought to have become a Jain after the Jain sage Bhadrabaku correctly predicted a twelve-year famine. Overcome by the tragedy, Chandragupta spent his last days with Bhadrabaku and fasted to death.

Chandragupta Maurya entertains his Persian-Seleucid bride, a daughter of Seleucus I Nicator. Their marriage confirmed peace between the Mauryas and the Seleucids.

THE MAURYAS

Bindusara, Chandragupta's son, reigned from about 297 BCE to 273 BCE, expanding the empire south and conquering the Deccan in western and southern India. He developed peaceful relations with the territories of the extreme south and with the Hellenic world.

A war of succession followed Bindusara's death, ending with his son Ashoka taking the throne. Reigning from about 275 to 232 BCE, he was the last Mauryan emperor.

THE BUDDHIST EMPEROR

A seated Buddha on one of the stupas at Sanchi, built by King Ashoka near Vidisha.

After a very bloody struggle to win the Kalinga territory in southern India, Ashoka was horrified by the suffering caused. Becoming a convinced Buddhist, he renounced war, instead perpetrating "conquest by dharma." By dharma he meant a broad concept of tolerance, compassion, non-violence, and good works. He gave all religions freedom to practice, and undertook tours of preaching in rural areas where he also tried to relieve local suffering.

Government officials were commanded to be aware of the needs of the common people and to be impartial in dispensing justice. A whole class of officers known as dharma ministers was set up to to alleviate suffering in general and in particular to look after the needy people: women, those living on the outskirts of the empire, and those outside its borders. Ashoka ended forced and indentured labor.

He founded hospitals for both people and animals, built rest houses and wells, watersheds, monasteries, and stupas.

Ashoka ordered that he be informed of all matters of public welfare, stating that he sought only the glory of leading his people along the path of dharma. His own son and daughter were missionaries in Sri Lanka, and missionaries were sent as far as North Africa. Buddhism spread throughout India and beyond due to Ashoka's efforts.

Ashoka had rocks and pillars inscribed with his thoughts and his acts. Two of these were written in Greek, and one in Aramaic and Greek, although most were in the Prakrit language. The national emblem of India is the lion capital of one of these pillars at Sarnath.

Under Ashoka India experienced 50 years of peace. However, on his death his work was discontinued. Weaker kings ruled much reduced territory, with the empire disintegrating about 50 years after Ashoka, superseded by the Shunga dynasty.

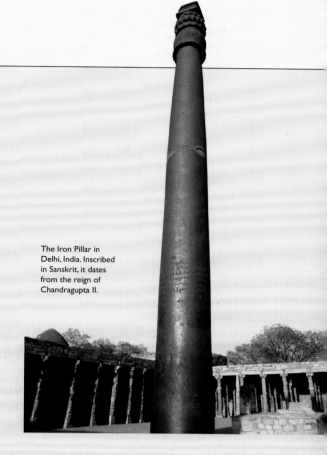

The Iron Pillar in Delhi, India. Inscribed in Sanskrit, it dates from the reign of Chandragupta II.

Carvings on the gate to the Great Stupa at Sanchi relate tales of King Ashoka's life.

The birthplace of the world's three great monotheistic religions, West Asia was once home to thousands of different gods and goddesses.

MESOPOTAMIA

Due to the nature of Mesopotamia's society, more than 1,000 deities existed, although one god or goddess could have many alternate names depending on their different manifestations. The main gods and goddesses worshipped were:

MARDUK

Marduk was the national god of Babylonia and the chief god of the city of Babylon. God of thunderstorms and with 50 names, each a divine attribute, he was later called "Bel," god of order and destiny. His consort was considered to be Zarpanitu. Marduk was often shown wearing a tunic covered with stars and carrying in his hand a scepter, or a bow, spear, net, or thunderbolt. The oldest depictions of Marduk show him in a war chariot, or holding a hoe/

Marduk, the chief god of Babylon.

triangular spade, a symbol of fertility and vegetation.

Marduk's sacred animals were horses, dogs, and a dragon with a forked tongue. Carvings of these animals were put on the city walls. He conquered Tiamat, the primordial dragon of chaos, to become Lord of the Gods of Heaven and Earth.

An Akkadian cylinder seal dating to about 2300 BCE shows the Sumerian god Enki (second on the right) with water erupting from his shoulder, while in the center the sun god Utu is emerging from the depths, below the winged goddess Inanna.

All kings, people, and nature owed him their existence and destiny.

The main temple to Marduk in Babylon was Esgila, and the Etemenanki, a ziggurat, had a shrine to Marduk on the summit.

INANNA

Inanna was the most important Sumerian goddess and queen of the land. A fertility goddess, she filled the world's rivers and springs with her "blood." Every king was said to be her bridegroom. The Hittites called her Inaras. More myths were told about Inanna than about any other deity, including the story of her descent into the underworld to challenge her older sister, Erishkigal, the queen of the dead.

ISHTAR

"Star" in Babylonian, also called Light of the World, goddess of war and love, Ishtar is the Great Goddess mentioned in the Bible as Ashtoreth, Asherah, Anath, and the Queen of Heaven. An Akkadian goddess of fertility, Ishtar was worshipped in the Middle East under many names and influenced the cults of other goddesses such as the Semitic goddess Astarte, as well as Cybele, Aphrodite, and the Goddess Har, the compassionate prostitute.

In Babylonian and Assyrian religion, Ishtar was the goddess of fertility. She was a form of the ancient Great Mother Goddess.

Nabu, the god of writing and therefore wisdom in Babylonian mythology.

Tower and arch on the site of the Temple of Sin, god of the moon, at Harran, Turkey.

The sun god Shamash on his throne within his shrine.

NABU

The god of writing and vegetation. The son of Marduk, Nabu was revered by the Babylonians and the Assyrians. His symbols were a clay tablet and a stylus. He is called "Nebo" in the Bible.

SIN

The Akkadian god of the moon and father of Shamash, Sin was also known as Nanna. His symbol was the crescent moon. He was often represented as an elderly man with a flowing beard, wearing four horns and a crescent moon on his head.

SHAMASH

The Akkadian god of the sun, Shamash was often depicted with a solar winged disc. Together with Sin and Ishtar, Shamash formed the Babylonian heavenly trinity of sun, moon, and stars. Shamash had the power of light over darkness and evil. With this he became the god of justice and equity over gods and humanity. At night, Shamash became the judge of the underworld. It was believed that Hammurabi received his Code of Law from Shamash. He was sometimes depicted sweeping across the heavens in a chariot, a boat, or on horseback.

CANAAN/SYRIA/THE LEVANT

Some of the old gods of this region were mentioned in the Bible.

BAAL

Baal was the god of fertility, so had many titles. He was often called Lord of the Earth, but in Phoenician he was called Lord of the Heavens. This reflects his aspect as a storm god, the Lord of Rain and Dew, which would have been crucial for agriculture in the region. He was sometimes called "He Who Rides on the Clouds."

A gold-covered bronze statue of the god Baal.

According to legend, Baal would have to fight Mot, the opposing god of death and sterility, to determine whether the world would enjoy a seven-year cycle of fertility or drought and famine.

IRAN

In the period before Zoroastrianism in Iran, Mithra was the sun god, and also represented justice, contract and obligation, and war. Known as Mithras in the Roman Empire, from 136 CE onwards he became the soldiers' god and was the center of a mystery cult. It was encouraged by emperors because Mithraism also included a sense of loyalty to the ruler. However when Christianity became encouraged in the Roman Empire his worship faded away.

Statue of Mithras, ancient Persian god of light who was adopted into the Roman pantheon.

"*We will develop and cultivate the liberation of mind by loving kindness, make it our vehicle, make it our basis, stabilize it, exercise ourselves in it, and fully perfect it.*"

– The Buddha

When the pampered, privileged, and protected Hindu prince Siddhartha Gautama left his family's royal compound for the first time in his life, he was appalled by the suffering he observed. A grown adult, he had never before seen illness, old age, or death.

When he learned that those are all unavoidable, and the inevitable fate of human beings, he embarked on a quest to understand more about human suffering.

Siddhartha Gautama was born in what is today Nepal possibly in 563 BCE, though some scholars now think it may have been later than this, around 490 BCE. He died either around 483 BCE or around 410 BCE.

A statue of the seated Buddha giving a gesture intended to banish fear. From a Chinese temple cave dating to the late 6th century or early 7th century CE.

Prince Siddhartha Gautama became a champion of swordplay, wrestling, and archery.

Prince Siddhartha first meets an old man and a sick man. A detail from a Chinese silk painting.

c.563 (or **c.490**) Birth of the Buddha.
c.483 (or **c.410**) Death of the Buddha.
c.260–232 Ashoka commissions the brick-built Great Stupa at Sanchi to hold a relic of the Buddha.

He decided to become a homeless monk, and sought wisdom from holy men. One advised him to practice asceticism, to live a life of strict discipline and self-denial. This brought Gautama no special understanding of self or suffering. Others advised him to meditate, but he found that even a deep meditative state did not enable him to escape the world of suffering. So he chose the Middle Way, neither asceticism nor luxury.

A sacred bodhi fig tree at Bodhgaya, India, a descendant of the tree under which the Buddha gained enlightenment.

ENLIGHTENMENT

One day, when meditating under a bo or bodhi fig tree in Bodhgaya near Patna, India, Gautama finally reached enlightenment, gaining an understanding of the true nature of existence. So he became the Buddha, "the Enlightened One" or "the Awakened One," and devoted the rest of his life to teaching others to also become enlightened.

His revelation freed him from the cycle of rebirth and earthly suffering which Hindus believe in, so that when he eventually died he escaped the material world and entered paradise, or the state of eternal bliss, known as Nirvana. Some of his followers also achieved enlightenment, but chose to be reborn on earth to help others. These became known as Bodhisattvas, or saints.

BUDDHIST BELIEFS

Buddhist beliefs can be summed up in the Four Noble Truths, also known as the law or the dharma:
- *Suffering is an inescapable part of life*
- *Suffering has a cause*
- *The cause is humanity's desire for change*
- *Suffering can be removed if desire can be removed*

And the Eight-fold Path which leads to the removal of desire:
- *Right Understanding and Right Thought (Wisdom)*
- *Right Speech, Right Action, and Right Livelihood (Ethical Conduct)*
- *Right Effort, Right Mindfulness, and Right Concentration (Mental Development)*

The practice of these virtues can lead to enlightenment, as experienced by the Buddha, and thus an escape from earthly suffering to Nirvana.

   Buddhism divided into many sects, some advocating total withdrawal from the mundane world, others recommending meditation or mantras (chants), or involving prayers for help addressed to various saints.

   Buddhism does not include the worship of gods, but is more a philosophy of life.

A Thai statue of the eighteen-armed Guanyin (Kwan Yin), the Buddhist representation of mercy, compassion, and protection.

Ancient Buddhist pagodas in the countryside near Bagan in Myanmar.

Buddhist missionaries spread out along the Silk Road or took ship along the coast in Southeast Asia. Buddhism often adapted itself to local religions, for example in China its temples became centers for ancestor veneration, and bodhisattvas such as Guanyin (Kwan Yin), the compassionate female protector figure, became popular deities worshipped in folk religion. Chan or Zen Buddhism, which involves deep meditation, originated in China and was quite similar to Daoism in the way it approached the universe. Meanwhile, Tibetan Buddhism developed in another direction, using prayer-wheels and mandalas (symbolic pictures), and emphasizing tantra or bodily development.

The site of Buddha's enlightenment is now the Mahabodhi Temple, housing a descendant of the bo tree the Buddha sat under. It is an important pilgrimage site. Other, sometimes very simple Buddhist buildings, are stupas or domed burial mounds where Buddhists can meditate about suffering and death.

159

THE RAMAYANA

The *Ramayana* is an epic poem narrating the divine Prince Rama's struggles to reclaim his wife Sita from the multi-headed demon king Ravana. Together with the *Mahabharata*, the *Ramayana* is the basis of early Hindu history.

Divided into seven books in 24,000 couplets, the *Ramayana* portrays several ideal characters and relationships:

- The ideal of conjugal love
- The ideal of brotherly love
- The ideal king
- The ideal kingdom

The *Ramayana* also contains many other myths and stories that typify exemplary behavior. Rama himself demonstrates dharma or the righteous path.

THE BOOKS

THE FIRST BOOK

Rama is one of four sons born to Dasharatha, Maharaja of Ayodhya, who had three wives. Each son had something of the essence of the god Vishnu, who had been born into humanity to combat the demon king Ravana. Ravana can only be defeated by a mortal. Aged sixteen, Rama is chosen by a sage to combat demons who have been disrupting sacrificial rites.

Rama and his brother Lakshmana receive supernatural powers and destroy the demons.

Janaka, the king of Mithila, decrees that whoever can wield the bow given to his ancestors by Shiva will receive the hand of his daughter Sita.

Rama lifts the bow and marries Sita, while his three brothers marry her three sisters.

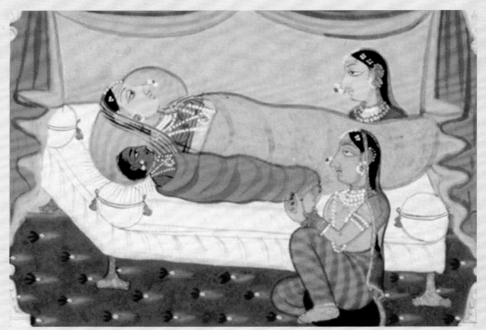

The birth of Rama in the royal palace at Ayodhya.

The earliest written text of the *Ramayana* is estimated to be from the 7th century BCE up till the 4th century BCE, with later stages of the text dated to the 3rd century BCE.

Rama is one of the most popular of Hindu deities. The purpose of his incarnation was to show us the righteous path or dharma, and reading or hearing the *Ramayana* is believed by many to impart blessings as well as freedom from sin.

c.500 Based on a much earlier oral tradition, the Indian epic poem the *Ramayana* is written down.

Scenes from the *Ramayana* are depicted on sculptures, paintings, and bronzes throughout India. The epic also had a profound affect on the literature and art of the entire Indian subcontinent as well as that of southeast Asia.

THE SECOND BOOK

After twelve years, Dasharatha proclaims his desire to crown Rama his heir. Preparations are made for Rama's coronation as Prince Regent, but Manthara, a wicked maid, poisons the mind of Kaikeyi, Dasharatha's second wife. Years before, Dasharatha had promised Kaikeyi two boons for saving his life, so she now demands that her son, Bharata, is made heir and that Rama should be banished for fourteen years. True to his word, Dasharatha reluctantly agrees. Rama accepts this decision humbly, and accompanied by Sita and his brother Lakshmana goes to live in the forest. Rama tries to persuade Sita to stay behind, but she insists that her place is with him. Griefstricken, Dasharatha dies. Reluctant to profit from the situation, Bharata places Rama's sandals on the throne, ruling as his regent.

The marriage of Rama and his three brothers to the four daughters of King Janaka.

THE THIRD BOOK

After thirteen years Rama, Sita, and Lakshmana settle by the banks of the river Godavari. They clash with the demon king Ravana's monstrous sister and Ravana abducts Sita. The brothers set out to search for her, meeting various people and demons along the way.

THE FOURTH BOOK

Rama and Lakshmana meet Hanuman, the monkey general, who learns that Sita is being held on an island, Lanka.

THE FIFTH BOOK

This is a detailed account of Hanuman's exploits. He assumes gigantic form and makes an enormous leap into Lanka where he meets demons and finds Sita, but she refuses to leave with him, saying Rama must avenge her.

Rama allows himself to be captured by Ravana, lecturing Ravana before he escapes.

THE SIXTH BOOK

This book tells the story of the war between Rama and Ravana, ending with Rama killing Ravana.

Rama asks Sita to undertake a test of fire to prove her chastity. Agni, Lord of fire, raises Sita unharmed from the fire.

They return to Ayodha, where Rama is crowned and rules a perfect kingdom with ideal morals.

Rama leaving for fourteen years of exile from Ayodhya.

The Battle at Lanka.

Meghnath (son of Ravana) render Rama and Lakshmana unconscience by using Nagpash (a magical weapon)

A wounded Lakshmana is tended by the doctor Sushen.

THE SEVENTH BOOK

The final book reinforces the notion of Rama as an avatar of Vishnu. Rama's actions have lasting significance, reinforcing the caste system, and ensuring the well-being of the Brahmins.

Lakshmana submits to the curse of the sage Durvasa, going voluntarily to his death. Rama doesn't intervene.

As a king, Rama must be above reproach, and rumors about Sita's purity because she had lived with another man cause him to banish her. Valmiki the sage gives her shelter in his hermitage in the forest, and there she bears Rama twin boys, Lava and Kusha, who grow up ignorant of their heritage.

Valmiki composes the *Ramayana* and teaches Lava and Kusha to sing it. Rama holds a ceremony during which the boys sing the *Ramayana*, and Rama is stricken with grief when he hears about Sita being exiled. Valmiki produces Sita, who calls upon her mother, the Earth, to receive her. The ground opens and she disappears, and Rama learns the identity of Lava and Kusha.

Years later, Rama receives a visit from a messenger of the gods, who tells him his time of incarnation is ended. Rama ascends to heaven to rejoin Vishnu.

Sita is saved from burning by Agni, the god of fire.

COMMENTARIES

Many academics believe that both the first and the last books are later additions to the text. It is in these books that it is explicitly stated that Rama is Vishnu, and, in accordance with later theology, that Vishnu takes human form. The final book also explains the events of earlier books and there we see lives being governed by past actions.

A Javanese wall relief depicting Rama.

The longest epic poem in the world, the *Mahabharata* consists of around 100,000 verses. Written in Sanskrit, its name means "great epic of the Bharata Dynasty." (Bharata Khanda was a term for India.)

The *Mahabharata* is a compendium of dharma, or the righteous path, demonstrating duties, rights, laws, conduct, and virtues. Vedic ritual, adoration of gods, and pilgrimages are covered in the text. Book 3, the Book of

The *Mahabharata* has inspired great art in many different forms.

the Forest, has sages teaching the heroes, while book 12, the Book of Peace, gives an account of moral matters.

A great battle between the Pandavas and their cousins, the Kauravas, sons of Dhritarashtra, is the focus of the poem.

Dhritarashtra is King of the Kurus, while the Pandavas are the five sons of Pandu and his two wives. Each family has a claimant to the throne of Hastinapura, the kingdom of the Kurus.

The Pandavas are ultimately victorious in the great battle of Kurukshetra, with the battle showing conflicts between friendship and kinship, and between duty and family loyalty. The text ends with the ascent of the Pandavas to heaven, and with the death of Krishna.

The text is the source of the early worship of Krishna, although he is not

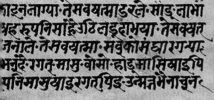

PANDAVAS AND DRAUPADI

All five Pandava brothers were married to the same one woman, Draupadi. Their actual fathers were various gods, since Pandu had been cursed to die if he had intercourse.

The five Pandava brothers with their wife Draupadi.

The Pandava and Kaurava armies face each other.

defined as a god throughout. Instead, he is a hero, not yet one of the most important incarnations of the god Vishnu. Krishna helps the Pandavas regain their kingdom, revealing the *Bhagavad Gita* and disclosing his status as the supreme deity. Krishna's story is further developed in tales of his youth, this theme having an important influence on art.

Shiva is also seen as a supreme god in many of the myths told, particularly in his battle with the hero Arjuna.

The *Bhagavad Gita*, part of the *Mahabharata*, is Hinduism's most significant religious text. Consisting of eighteen chapters, its name means "Song of God" and it outlines paths to self-realization, salvation, and liberation from ignorance and the cycle of rebirth. These paths include discipline of action, selflessness in doing good, ascetic withdrawal from the world into meditation and reflection, and the search for knowledge. It also discusses the discipline of devotion to a personal

In one of the many stories told in the *Mahabharata*, Dushasana attempts to humiliate Draupadi.

यदा यदा हि धर्मस्य ग्लानिर्भवती भारत ।
अभ्युत्थानमर्धमस्य तदाऽऽत्मनं सृजाम्यहम ।।

A scene from the *Bhagavad Gita* where Krishna enters battle along with Arjuna.

god, where seeking a vision of God through worship can enable release from the bonds of this world.

This new emphasis on worship remained important in Hinduism, while the Vedic gods were largely demoted.

While the *Mahabharata* is an exposition of dharma, or proper codes of conduct, it also shows that it is impossible not to violate these complex codes in some way. It raises the question of whether suffering caused by war can be justified. Just means, just causes, and just treatment of captives are all considered. The *Bhagavad Gita* also provides a strong justification for the caste system in its emphasis on various responsibilities assigned according to birth.

Overall, the *Mahabharata* is both a religious text and a history, although its central events are still debated. It is a significant text in the development of Hinduism between 400 BCE and 200 CE, a period when the transition from Vedic sacrifice to sectarian Hinduism took place, as did interaction with Buddhism and Jainism.

An administrative tablet from the Seleucid period showing the impression of a stamp seal.

The largest state to evolve out of Alexander the Great's empire, the Seleucid kingdom, founded in 312 BCE, continued the Hellenization of a wide area of West and Central Asia. Greek became the language of government, diplomacy, and literature, and Greek migrants settled throughout the region, bringing their culture and religion to urban areas. The city of Antioch in Syria was founded, and the province of Bactria in east Iran and north Afghanistan, where some of Alexander the Great's Macedonian soldiers had settled, became a major Greek settlement.

But Seleucus I Nicator, the first Seleucid emperor, quickly faced an erosion of his authority at the edges of the empire. In the Far East, Chandragupta Maurya was building his own empire in India, and was whittling away at Seleucid territories. In 305 Seleucus agreed to give Chandragupta most of the territory that Alexander the Great had struggled to win in the Indian subcontinent, including the Hindu Kush, covering much of modern-day Afghanistan and eastern Pakistan. In return Seleucus received a number of war elephants to bolster his forces in the west.

Under Seleucus's successors, more regions such as Cappadocia in Anatolia, Bithynia, Pontus, and Pergamum all broke away and soon were effectively

Seleucus I Nicator, one of Alexander the Great's generals who took control of Alexander's territories in West Asia and founded the Seleucid Empire.

Antiochus III "the Great" of the Seleucid Empire.

independent. Then the Central Asian polities of Bactria, Sogdiana, and Parthia splintered off. The Seleucids did not enjoy many periods of peace. They were often at war with the Ptolemies to the west, and regularly campaigned to bring breakaway provinces back under control, with varying degrees of success.

Just as the Parthian Empire was growing in strength in northeastern Iran, in 190 BCE, under Antiochus III, the Great, the Seleucids overextended by trying to reclaim Alexander the Great's Greek territories. This brought them into conflict with the growing power of Rome, and they were decimated by the Romans at the Battle of Magnesia. As reparation Antiochus lost all of his lands in Anatolia west of the Taurus. As the Parthians in the east of the empire began to expand, the Seleucids were reduced to a rump state in Syria until the Roman general Pompey finally ended the dynasty in 64 BCE.

312 The Seleucid Empire is founded, controlling most of the Asian parts of Alexander the Great's empire.

c.300 The Seleucids found the city of Antioch in Syria.

300 The Seleucids of Persia move Greek soldiers and colonizers into Bactria in modern Afghanistan, where some of Alexander the Great's soldiers have already settled.

261 Greeks in Bactria, Afghanistan, break away from the Seleucids and declare an independent Hellenistic state, which grows to reach from Turkmenistan to the Punjab

c.200 The Greco–Persian Seleucids defeat Egypt and take control of Syria and Judah.

late 2nd century Jewish refugees fleeing from the Seleucid king Antiochus Epiphanes might have settled in India.

190 Battle of Magnesia: Rome defeats the Seleucids of Persia and Roman client states take lands in Anatolia west of the Taurus.

166 The Hasmonean revolt begins against Seleucid rule in Judah.

142 Judah wins independence from the Seleucids.

129 Collapse of the Seleucid Empire. Parthians take over Babylonia.

64 Rome absorbs the final parts of the Seleucid Empire in Syria and Lebanon into the Roman Empire.

The Battle of Magnesia in 190 BCE, the concluding battle of the Roman–Seleucid War.

One of the most authoritarian political philosophies ever invented, the Chinese philosophy of Legalism, developed in the 4th century BCE, held that a ruler must be strong and firm, and has absolute power to enforce the law. The legal code should be known to everyone and strictly obeyed, and lawbreakers should be harshly punished. The ruler should have complete authority.

The Legalists believed that this was the only way to create a strong state, since human beings are driven by selfishness

THE FIRST EMPEROR

Qin was the only major faction in the Chinese Warring States Period (475–221 BCE) that did not suffer from civil wars. It was also a relatively new state, so instead of relying on long-established feudal practices, the Qin rulers could create their own system of government. But it was never one of the major powers until the adoption of Legalism.

When the Legalist bureaucrat Shang Yang (390–338 BCE) left the kingdom of Wei in search of a state in which he could apply his ideas, he found the perfect match in Qin, whose ruler, Xiao, was perfectly happy to strengthen his authority. Together they reformed Qin into a smoothly running, well-organized machine.

First, of course, they stressed the rule of law and royal decree. But by insisting that laws should apply to all, whatever their status, Shang Yang began to offend the old aristocracy. He then convinced Xiao to award nobility only to those who earned it by working for the state, especially in battle. He introduced centrally appointed governors, standard weights and measures, compulsory military service, and gave incentives for agricultural production.

Qin's prosperity grew, but after Xiao's death Shang Yang faced a gruesome death at the hands of disgruntled lords.

From then on Qin began its climb to ascendancy, using espionage, assassination, bribery, and a policy of divide-and-rule. Legalism was not forgotten, however, as in 247 BCE the Legalist Li Si also took service

in Qin. The philosophy was eagerly adopted by Zheng, who inherited the Qin kingdom when he was just thirteen and would go on to become China's First Emperor, Qin Shi Huangdi.

China's first imperial dynasty was also its shortest, lasting for just two emperors and 15 years, from 221 to 207 BCE, but leaving behind two of the world's great cultural legacies: the Terracotta Army and part of China's Great Wall.

Earlier rulers had used the title of king (wang), and the chaotic Warring States Period saw China fragment into

Qin Shi Huangdi, king of the Chinese state of Qin and China's "First Emperor."

and short-term self-interest, so need to be strictly controlled. They thought that the goal of the people should be to increase the power of the state and its ruler. The philosophy supported a strict doctrine of obedience, efficiency, and hard work.

Bronze crossbow from, Eastern Zhou dynasty.

several small kingdoms, meaning that "king" became an overused title. So the man who reunified the Chinese state took for himself a grander title, that of emperor. Although his dynasty did not last long, the imperial system that this First Emperor established was to last for more than 2,000 years, giving China the longest continuous culture in the world.

The First Emperor's original name was Zhao Zheng or Ying Zheng. He was born around 259 BCE in the state of Qin, which was centered in the modern province of Shaanxi in north-western China and was already becoming one of the most powerful of the Warring States.

Zheng's mother was the former concubine of a powerful merchant, Lu Buwei, who, for financial purposes, schemed to make Zheng's father, Zhuangxiang, king of Qin.

In 246 BCE, Zheng inherited the kingdom aged just thirteen, but he was powerless until he organized a palace coup when he came of age in 238 BCE. He immediately exiled Lu Buwei, who had been acting as head of state, had his mother's current lover executed, and continued Qin's military campaigns. He very soon made his personality clear when he ordered the deaths of prisoners of war, and in 221 BCE his wars of conquest were complete. He declared himself Emperor of China.

The title adopted by Zheng, Qin Shi Huangdi, literally means First (Shi) Qin Emperor (Huangdi). Although the earlier Shang and Zhou dynasties did rule over several unified kingdoms, their rulers called themselves kings. The title of emperor had been reserved for the mythical rulers of the distant past, such as the legendary Yellow Emperor, who was said to have brought many of the trappings of civilization to China.

But Qin Shi Huangdi believed in hubris rather than humility, and claimed for himself the same title as the great mythical figures of the past. Cruel, tyrannical, and increasingly paranoid, he had huge palaces built – along with an extraordinary, grandiose tomb – and lived as if he was himself a semi-divine, legendary figure. He survived at least three assassination attempts, and to avoid other attacks he would sleep in a different room every night.

THE FIRST EMPEROR

Together with Li Si, Shi Huangdi created a strong, centralized bureaucratic government and military organization. They abolished the feudal states and replaced them with regions governed by a centrally appointed official, standardized coins, weights, and measures, and, of course, demanded strict obedience to the Emperor's decrees. He even dictated how wide carts should be.

He thought nothing of forming huge, conscript gangs to work on projects such as roads, or his tomb, or the Great Wall, and he introduced a harsh system of punishments for lawbreakers, including mutilation, castration, branding, and brutal methods of execution.

The Legalist philosopher and bureaucrat Li Si.

THE BURNING OF THE BOOKS

Shi Huangdi was especially interested in the alchemists' search for the elixir of immortality, but when he summoned magicians to his court, Confucian scholars scoffed at the whole idea. It is reported that Shi Huangdi executed 460 scholars for their contempt, then, at the urging of Li Si, he ordered all books outside his own imperial library that were not about agriculture, medicine, some forms of divination, or historical records to be burnt. Only a few classic books escaped the conflagration. It is possible, however, that this is one of the many stories that later grew up about his tyrannical behaviour, and that he only had the books kept away from public use.

Qin Shi Huangdi burning books and killing scholars.

About a hundred years after the First Emperor's death, the Chinese historian Sima Qian (145–90 BCE) described how the tomb was built:

"They dug down deep to underground springs, pouring copper to place the outer casing of the coffin. Palaces and

viewing towers housing a hundred officials were built and filled with treasures and rare artifacts. Workmen were instructed to make automatic crossbows primed to shoot at intruders. Mercury was used to simulate the hundred rivers, the Yangtze and Yellow River, and the great sea, and set to flow mechanically. The Second Emperor said: 'It is inappropriate for the wives of the late emperor who have no sons to be free,' ordered that they should accompany the dead, and a great many died. After the burial, it was suggested that it would be a serious breach if the craftsmen who constructed the tomb and knew of its treasure were to divulge those secrets. Therefore, after the funeral ceremonies had completed, the inner passages and doorways were blocked, and the exit sealed, immediately trapping the workers and craftsmen inside. None could escape. Trees and vegetation were then planted on the tomb mound such that it resembled a hill."

Until the Terracotta Army was found accidentally by farmers in the 1970s, no one thought that Sima Qian's outlandish claims could be true. But this unexpected, extraordinary expression of Qin Shi Huangdi's hubris perhaps suggests that there are other great discoveries to be made in the necropolis. So far, we do not know. Only a fraction of the huge tomb has yet been excavated, so who knows what wonders might still remain under the mound and fields of the First Emperor's resting place.

A statue of Qin Shi Huangdi near his tomb at Xi'an.

THE QIN TOMB

Almost as soon as he inherited the throne of Qin, Shi Huangdi began work on his tomb. But it was not until he was emperor of China, in 219 BCE, that he ordered major construction work on his grandiose mausoleum. Carved out of a mountain near Xi'an, the site covered about 20 square miles (50 square km), with his huge coffin buried beneath a 249-foot-tall (76 meter) earth mound dominating the complex.

Shi Huangdi was not buried alone. In the west of his huge necropolis was the burial ground of the workers who had been forced to build the mausoleum, and in another area, the "stables," horses were buried next to terracotta figures of their grooms. The necropolis contained several traps to protect against tomb-robbers, and it is thought that the builders who were unlucky enough to be working on these ended up in the grave themselves, possibly walled up alive.

THE TERRACOTTA ARMY

Standing guard nearly a mile (about 1.5 km) east of the central tomb mound, the famous Terracotta Army was buried in huge pits. Created to serve the emperor in the afterlife, this "spirit army" consisted of some 8,000 life-size, terracotta sculptures of soldiers, together with 400 terracotta horses and 100 chariots, all arranged in battle formation.

The sculptures were built out of separate parts – heads, arms, legs, and torsos – made in molds then assembled, painted all over, and placed in their rows. About 30 different models of realistically detailed heads were used, but each figure was given more individuality by being hand-finished with extra clay so they all look slightly different. The emperor controlled everything: each workshop was made to put its mark on its sculptures, so every figure could be traced back to where it was made.

The statues of the Terracotta Army were originally brightly painted then lacquered, but with exposure to air the pigments and lacquer quickly flaked off, meaning that most of the surviving figures today appear plain terracotta. They were equipped with real weapons, many of which have been looted or rotted away, but some of those that have survived still have their sharp edges.

Although there is plenty of variety among the uniforms, the Terracotta Army basically consists of just a few general types:

- *Armored soldiers*
- *Unarmored infantrymen*
- *Cavalrymen*
- *Semi-armored chariot drivers*
- *Spear-carrying chariot riders*
- *Armored kneeling archers*
- *Unarmored standing archers*

And, of course, the officers. Qin Shi Huangdi's ideas of a strict social hierarchy extended to his spirit army. The more important the soldier, the taller the sculpture, so the officers were taller than the ordinary soldiers, and the generals in the separate command post were taller still.

It is thought that all in all about 700,000 conscripts worked on the tomb.

The whole complex was built to mirror the hierarchical arrangement of Shi Huangdi's real capital city. So, surrounding his tomb were terracotta figures of courtiers and court officials, as well as a number of bronze chariots and horses. Then an inner wall was built, outside of which the imperial park was reconstructed, with bronze statues of musicians as well as various birds such as swans and cranes. This area also contained terracotta figures of court entertainers.

Around this an outer wall was built, outside which were other distinct but less important sections, such as offices and the stables.

THE QIN GREAT WALL

Most of the surviving Great Wall of China was built by the Ming dynasty (1368–1644 CE) , but the first walls were built much earlier, mainly in the Yellow River valley and northern China areas, during the Spring and Autumn and Warring States periods, when many states fought against each other and against northern raiders. Small sections of these walls do survive.

The walls were not just defenses against horsemen from the north; they also blocked raiders from easily carrying any loot north again, they were territorial markers, and they made a statement about the builders' power and strength.

Under Shi Huangdi, the Qin embarked on the first major period of wall-building. Several hundred thousand workers (or prisoners) were conscripted to strengthen the existing series of walls along the northern border, connect up the various different earthworks, and to extend them. Over the course of about ten years, he covered 1,500 miles (2,400 km) from modern Liaoning

The Great Wall of China near Beijing.

Province in the east to the Inner Mongolian Desert.

The Qin Great Wall was a complex including garrison stations and signal towers. As with later dynasties, the builders used natural features of the landscape to help the fortification – narrow passes, steep mountains, and deep gorges were all incorporated into the design to make the wall more of a barrier.

The earliest walls on the plains were just compacted earth, sometimes mixed with a small amount of gravel to add solidity. They were built by filling a simple wooden frame with earth that was then tamped into a compact layer. Another frame was put on top, and so, layer by layer, the walls rose. Rammed earth like this could withstand weapons such as arrows, swords, and spears, but in mountainous areas unshaped stones were simply piled up to form a barrier.

Now one of the architectural wonders of the world, the Great Wall of China is the longest structure ever built, twisting and turning for 4,163 miles (6,700 km) across north China. So many millions of workers died during its construction that it is called the longest cemetery in the world.

END OF THE QIN

Qin Shi Huangdi boasted that his dynasty would last 10,000 generations, while in fact it did not even survive two. After his death in 210 BCE his sons struggled between themselves for power but faced rebellion from all sides. In the first place, sensing weakness, members of the ruling families of conquered states began to try to reassert their local authority. Secondly, huge numbers of soldiers had deserted, forming bandit armies that undermined the state's military control. Finally, the Qin heirs faced the first popular uprisings by Chinese peasants. In the end it was one of these peasant leaders, Liu Bang, who defeated the Qin and founded a great dynasty in 206 BCE, the Han.

LEGACY

Shi Huangdi had held the empire together partly because of his forceful personality. His successor was a much weaker character, unable to impose his will on the old feudal factions or to control the popular uprisings. The Qin dynasty collapsed and the remaining members of the imperial family were killed in 206 BCE.

The succeeding dynasty, the Han, adopted Confucianism and demonized Legalism, so emphasized the brutal aspects of Shi Huangdi's reign. He was cruel and despotic, but the bureaucratic and

CHINA AND SINO

Qin was spelled Ch'in in the older style of transliteration, which gives its name to the word "China." The Arab version, Sin, is thought to be the root of the Latinized prefix "Sino-," meaning "Chinese," and the word "Sinology," for the study of China.

administrative structure that he created remained the basis of all future dynasties in China.

Throughout history the vast majority of rulers, generals, religious leaders, and politicians were men. So, it was their thoughts and actions that history – also usually written by men – recorded.

The lives and achievements of women were often ignored.

In ancient Asia, even women who had an important part to play might not have their names recorded. For example, some

PUABI OF UR

Either a priestess or a member of the royal family in the Sumerian city of Ur, Puabi is known because of her magnificent tomb.

Her skeleton shows that she was not quite five feet (1.5 m) tall and she died when she was about 40 years old. It is thought she lived around 2500 BCE, just before the first dynasty of Ur.

Puabi was so important in life that in death several servants were sacrificed to join her in her tomb. These included bodyguards and maids, as well as a horse and some lions. Her grave was not disturbed by tomb robbers, so the treasures which were buried with her were found intact. These included an ornate golden headdress, gold, silver, carnelian, and lapis lazuli jewelry, a chariot with silver trappings, a lyre, and gold tableware.

Puabi of Ur.

KUBABA OF SUMER

The first recorded female ruler in history, Kubaba, Queen of Sumer around 2400 BCE, was the only woman on the Sumerian King List.

Some chronicles say she was the only ruler of her dynasty, while others record that the House of Kubaba included her son and grandson succeeding her as the fourth dynasty of Kish.

According to one chronicle, Kubaba was working in a tavern when, because of her piety, the god Marduk, the protector of Babylon, ordained that she should have "sovereignty over the whole world." Her reign was one of peace and prosperity, and she later became the tutelary goddess who protected the city of Carchemish.

Queen Kubaba of Sumer.

ENHEDUANNA OF AKKAD

The world's first named writer, Enheduanna was a poet and priestess born in Mesopotamia about 2285 BCE. Her father was Sargon of Akkad, the first person known to create an empire, and her mother was possibly a priestess from Sumeria in the south of Mesopotamia.

Enheduanna became a priestess of the moon god Nanna in the city of Ur, but two of her surviving five works are hymns in praise of the goddess Inanna. "Like the light of the rising moon, how she was sumptuously attired!" she wrote, and "(To) my lady wrapped in beauty, (to) Inanna!"

Another work is a collection of hymns dedicated to sacred temples in general.

It is thought that as princess, priestess, and poet Enheduanna may have inspired the Mesopotamian tradition of listing names of high priestesses. She died in 2250.

c.2400 BCE The first known female ruler is Queen Kubaba of Sumer.

c.2285–50 Life of the first named author, Akkadian poet and priestess Enheduanna (Sargon's daughter).

811–06 Five-year reign of the only female Assyrian queen, Sammu-ramat or Semiramis, as regent for her son.

c.76–67 Rule of the Hasmonean queen Salome Alexandra in Judea, a Golden Age for the Jews.

c.267 CE Queen Zenobia of Palmyra builds the Palmyrene Empire and later rebels against Rome.

c.272 Zenobia is captured by Rome. The end of the Palmyrene Empire.

An ancient Sumerian bas-relief portrait depicting Enheduanna.

Fu Hao, the First Female War Leader

Lady Fu Hao was one of 64 wives of the Chinese Emperor Wu Ding (ruled c.1250–1192 BCE), under whom the Shang dynasty reached its peak. She was the only ancient Chinese female general – the world's first – and also, unusually for women, a priestess who carried out sacrifices and controlled her own estate.

Leading an army of 13,000 soldiers, Fu Hao defeated one of the Shang's persistent enemies and negotiated a peace treaty. Her achievements are mentioned on oracle bones of the time, and she is also known from her tomb in Anyang, the last Shang capital. Although it was relatively small by the standards of the Shang royals, her tomb was still incredibly lavish, and since it was the only royal tomb that was not robbed, it gives a glimpse into the Shang world and the riches that were poured on their ruling family.

Dating to about 1200 BCE , Fu Hao's tomb measured 18 feet (5.6 m) by 13 feet (4 m) and contained 468 bronze objects, 775 jade objects, and more than 6,880 cowrie shells that were used as money. Below her lacquered coffin six dogs were buried, and around the edges of the grave pit 16 human skeletons were found, possibly servants who were sacrificed to serve her..

Lady Fu Hao.

DEBORAH, JUDGE OF ISRAEL

"Judge" was a title for a leader of the people of Israel. According to tradition, the prophet Deborah was a judge from 1107 BCE until she died in 1067 BCE, although different archeologists place her about a hundred years either side of that date.

In the Bible Deborah shows how the Canaanites can be defeated at Mount Tabor and also celebrates a victory over them.

The Jewish judge Deborah celebrating victory with a triumphal song.

of the Chinese princesses who were married to Xiongnu nomadic horsemen in order to cement peace treaties were not named by the historians, although the names of their Xiongnu husbands might be written down.

On the other hand, in Sumeria the role of high priestesses was thought to be so important that, just as in the King List, there was a list of their names, if not always of their works. So, despite the odds, some strong, clever women did make their mark and affect the course of the ancient world. These included the world's first named author and the first known female general.

SEMIRAMIS

Sammu-ramat, known to the Greeks as Semiramis, was the only woman to rule the Assyrian Empire, although she did so as regent for her son in 811 BCE. Her husband had had to struggle against his rebellious older brother, so the kingdom she inherited was weak and divided. Semiramis stabilized Assyria, went on campaign with her young son (unusually for a woman), and – as is shown by stelae of the time – earned the respect of the people before handing over power when her son came of age five years later. A stela from the town of Assur was dedicated to "Sammu-ramat, Queen of Shamshi-Adad, King of the Universe, King of Assyria; Mother of Adad-nirari, King of the Universe, King of Assyria."

From then on Semiramis entered legend. Many centuries later, Greek writers such as Herodotus and Diodorus romanticized her story. They made several historically impossible claims, stating that she founded the city of Babylon and invaded India. The truth is that she was remembered for strengthening and reuniting the kingdom, and for being a female ruler.

Semiramis of Assyria and the Hanging Gardens of Babylon.

Artemisia I, Queen of Halicarnassus

Artemesia commanded five ships in the Persian fleet under Xerxes that invaded Greece in 480 BCE. The Greek historian Herodotus recorded that she fought well, despite the defeat at the naval Battle of Salamis, and that she then advised Xerxes to make a strategic withdrawal.

She ruled not just Halicarnassus (present-day Bodrum in Turkey), but also the islands of Nisyrus, Calymnos, and Cos. It was a later queen of the same name who raised the Mausoleum at Halicarnassus that was one of the Seven Wonders of the Ancient World.

Artemisia of Halicarnassus.

SALOME ALEXANDRA

In 142 BCE the Hasmonean or Maccabean family led the Jews of Judah to independence from the Greco–Persian Seleucids. But the Hasmonean kings ended up violent and corrupt. Then, in 76 BCE Salome Alexandra, widow of King Alexander Janneus, became queen and presided over a short Golden Age. She unified the country, ended civil war, and strengthened the nation by allowing the Pharisees, the religious party of ordinary people, to become part of the Sanhedrin, the religious tribunals previously run by the Sadducees, or Temple priests.

Salome Alexandra's social reforms included compulsory primary education for all children. She was well aware that Judah was surrounded by powerful, hungry nations, so all her efforts were intended to build up the nation into a stronger, united state.

Salome Alexandra.

When she died in 63 BCE her unifying influence died too. Civil war broke out between her two sons, both appealed to Rome for help, and instead of just providing aid to one or the other, Rome annexed the weakened country.

ZENOBIA

A militant and ambitious queen of the wealthy trading city of Palmyra in Syria, Zenobia declared independence from the Roman Empire in 269 CE and expanded her kingdom into an empire. She directed her army herself from horseback.

Rome struck back, however, and Zenobia was captured by Emperor Aurelian in 272. She was paraded in gold chains through the city of Rome, but was permitted to live, and she later married a Roman senator.

Queen Zenobia addressing her soldiers.

A thorn in the Chinese side for about 300 years, the nomadic Xiongnu horsemen from the Mongolian steppes formed a large confederacy from 209 BCE to 93 CE, regularly raiding China and disrupting the societies in Central Asia. The first stretches of wall in China were built to try and stop raids from the Xiongnu, but they were only partly effective. Strong raiding parties could bypass the walls or even overrun them. As well as walls, the Chinese tried punitive expeditions, treaties, and marriage alliances – nothing helped for long.

In the 2nd century BCE the Xiongnu looked west and raided the Yuezhi pastoralists. In turn, the Yuezhi moved off in search of pastures new, migrated to the west, then south through Bactria, defeating the Greco–Bactrians, and on to northwest India. There they eventually formed the Kushan Empire.

c.209 BCE Some of the nomadic Hunnish clans of Mongolia unite as the Xiongnu confederacy and begin regular raids into China.

c.200 China attempts to crush the Mongolian Xiongnu but is defeated. The two states divide their territory at the Great Wall.

c.150 The Xiongnu cross the Great Wall and take control of China north of the Yellow River.

c.121 China repels the Xiongnu and pushes them north of the Gobi desert.

48 CE The Xiongnu confederacy in Mongolia weakens and divides.

Eventually after a series of civil wars and facing a newly determined China, the Xiongnu confederation broke up. Some of the northern tribes migrated westward, and centuries later, it is thought they might have been some of the Huns, led by Attila, who terrorized Europe in the 5th century BCE.

A statue entitled 'Horse Stepping on a Xiongnu Soldier' stands on the tomb of General Huo Qubing, who died in 117 BCE. General Huo won a major victory over the Xiongnu.

Liu Bang, who overthrew the tyrannical Qin dynasty in 206 BCE, named his new dynasty Han and took the title of the Gaozu emperor. He copied the centralized administrative system of the Qin appointing officials to govern districts, but unlike the Qin he encouraged scholarship and cultural knowledge. The Han continued to use the Qin's standardized weights, measures, and coins.

Turning their backs on the totalitarian philosophy of Legalism, the Han adopted Confucianism. This still stressed obedience and knowing one's place in the social order, but it also emphasized filial piety and individual virtue. Emperor Wu, who reigned from 140 to 87 BCE, set up a university in the capital, Chang'an (modern Xi'an) to teach Confucian principles and conduct examinations for government officials. From then on, instead of being appointed regardless of ability, anyone seeking public office had to pass the Confucian exam. The civil service system of scholar-bureaucrats that the Han devised lasted throughout imperial China.

From their capital at Chang'an, the Han expanded their sphere of influence over most of modern China, and also

The triumphal entry of Han emperor Liu Bang into the imperial capital of Chang'an, 202 BCE.

became deeply influential throughout East Asia. It was a dynamic period during which several important advances were made in science and technology. Paper was

THE HAN GREAT WALL

Like most dynasties, the Han built new walls and extensions to the existing Great Wall, particularly to cover new trade routes in the west. In the modern-day region of Xinjiang alone they built about 600 miles (965 km) of wall.

The Han emperors extended the Wall across the deserts in the west of China. With typical ingenuity, the builders responded to this challenging terrain by building a moat, rather than a wall, but still with regular wooden beacon towers.

In dry desert lands the workers used a mixture of water, earth, and fine gravel reinforced with reeds, willow, and twigs of any available bushes. The mix was then tamped solid in a wooden frame, and left to dry. When the wooden frame was then removed, it left a solid slab of strengthened earth.

Han builders raised watchtowers at intervals of between 15 and 30 miles (24 to 48 km), and sent coded smoke signals, which were faster than messengers on horseback, to communicate between the towers. They used any local materials they could find for the fires, including wolf dung in some areas.

c.206 Liu Bang establishes the Han dynasty in China, becoming Emperor.

c.200 Under the Han dynasty silk becomes one of China's major exports, reaching Egypt and Rome.

25 CE The New Eastern Han dynasty overthrows the Qin in China.

Liu Bang, who overthrew the Qin and founded the Han Dynasty.

invented, the world's first seismograph was built, astronomical calendars were regularly improved, and water clocks and sundials were used. Trade along the Silk Roads began, and Sima Qian wrote an important history chronicle, *Records of the Grand Historian*. Future dynasties looked back on the Han with admiration and tried to emulate their achievements.

Part of the Great Wall of China built during the Han Dynasty.

ANCIENT CHINA ENDS

Some historians consider that the Han was the last of the ancient Chinese dynasties. The line weakened and several local military leaders began to emerge, until in 220 CE the Han dynasty gave way to the Three Kingdoms, another period of conflict and instability.

A jade figurine from the Western Han period thought to represent a grieving man.

Carvings on the wall of a tomb in Shandong show the artistic styles of the Han period.

A wine jar dating to the Han period showing a hunting scene in relief.

191

IMPERIAL SYMBOLS

For more than 2,000 years, until imperial China ended in 1911, the same symbols were used in China to represent imperial power. From the days of the Han, the dragon, a powerful, intelligent, dynamic, brave, and heroic creature, symbolized the emperor. It was the ultimate masculine or "yang" symbol, and also represented renewal. Along with other symbols such as the sun or moon for wisdom, grain for supplying food to his people, an ax to

A wooden carving of a crane (or possibly a phoenix) from the Eastern Han period.

HAN CHINESE ARTS

Many fine Chinese crafts developed from grave goods and tomb decorations. The elaborate bronze vessels of the Shang period, early jade carvings, and pottery models or "spirit-figures" were all either placed in tombs or used in religious ceremonies, usually to do with ancestor worship.

Large hanging scrolls originated in the banners that were hung in tombs from the Han dynasty onwards. The first major stone tomb sculpture was created in the Han period, when pottery house models were also placed in tombs. Under the Han, clay figurines of people and animals became particularly realistic and lifelike. Two of the main genres of Chinese painting, portraits and birds-and-flowers (which included all animal subjects) were first known as tomb decorations.

The third main genre of painting, landscape, was known under the Han but developed fully in the following period.

Chinese ceramics boasts a long history. By the time of the Longshan Culture about 4000 BCE, not only were potters using the wheel, but they had also developed distinctive patterns including the tripoidal shape that was mirrored in the Shang bronzes, and reflected yet

again in future periods. Glazing, a mineral coating that gives pots the valuable quality of being waterproof, was introduced under the Han. Over time the glaze became part of the art form, as different elements were added to produce subtle shades or bright colours, and either dull or iridescent effect.

As far back as 3000 years ago, in the Zhou dynasty, there were regulations about the use of lacquer. But it was under the Han that lacquer work was perfected, and used for exquisite decoration on a wide range of goods: from carriages to bows and arrows, food bowls, wine cups, and ceremonial vessels.

As silk became a major trade item under the Han, silk weaving developed into a full industry. Rich colours were used for the material and patterns of geometric designs or themes of clouds and mountains became popular.

The Han kept copious records, so we know about other arts such as metalwork, instrument-making, poetry, and creative writing. But for the Chinese, the most important and respected art form was calligraphy. By varying the brushstrokes and making each written character a piece of art in its own right,

Dragon statue style in Chinese temple.

represent authority, the imperial dragon would be embroidered on the emperor's clothes, used on his banner, and be a major part of palace decorations. The emperor's dragons had five claws, while a four-clawed dragon indicated a prince, and three claws stood for an imperial officer.

Similarly, the phoenix symbolized the empress. A sacred and spiritual creature, the phoenix is a mythological bird that periodically dies in a burst of flame but is renewed and reborn from its own ashes. It therefore shows the favor of heaven, and also represents happiness, beauty, peace, luck, and prosperity.

a calligrapher could show that his brush was moving in harmony with the universe, inspiring the imagination and mind of the reader with beauty and morality. Brushstrokes had picturesque and evocative names, such as "dragon-vein" or "rain-drop," meant to express an aspect of nature.

A bronze sculpture from the Han period of a pixiu or bixie mythological beast that was thought to ward off evil spirits.

The Roman historian Justin, who flourished in the 3rd century CE, wrote in bewilderment that the Parthians were "the most obscure of all the people of the East." To the great powers such as Greece and Rome, it must have seemed that the Parthian Empire appeared out of nowhere when it rose to take over most of the remaining provinces of the Seleucid Empire in the 2nd century BCE.

Also known as the Arsacids after Arsaces I, the leader of the Central Asian Parni tribe who first conquered the Parthian region of northeastern Iran, the Parthians began to expand their territory under Mithridates I, who ruled from about 171 to 138 BCE. He defeated the Greek colony of Bactria, then seized the old lands of Media and Mesopotamia from the Seleucids and took tribute from other kingdoms in Iran.

In the east Parthians claimed to rule lands as far as the Indus River, but experienced one of the major disruptions of the time as nomads were forced westwards

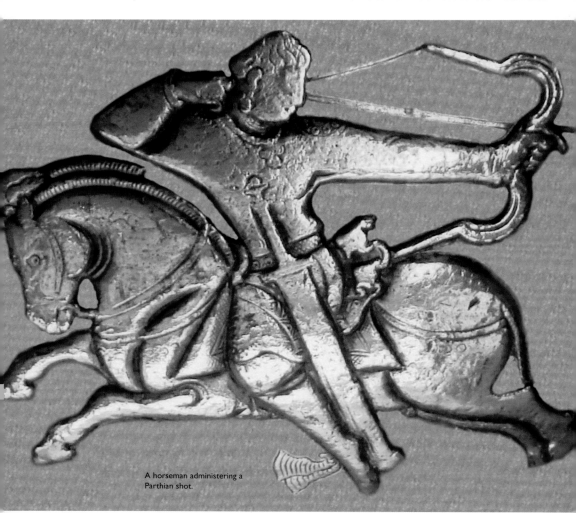

A horseman administering a Parthian shot.

when the Xiongnu confederation north of China began to expand. Parthia had to repulse an invasion by Scythians, known locally as the Saka.

Although the Seleucids fought back under Demetrius II Nicator in 140 BCE, he was eventually captured by the Parthians. From then on Parthia took the rest of the Babylonian territories and the Seleucids were reduced to a small area in Syria until conquered by the Romans in 64 BCE.

Controlling part of the Silk Road between China and the West, the Parthians grew rich from taxing trade caravans and from selling their own fruits, perfumes, and spices to merchants traveling along the Silk Road. Silk, pearls, iron, spices, and glassware all passed through Parthia. As a gesture of goodwill, in 87 CE Pacorus II of Parthia sent some exotic animals – lions and gazelles – to Emperor Zhang of the Han dynasty of China.

c.300 BCE Nomadic Parthians move into West Asia from the north.
c.129 Collapse of the Seleucid Empire. Parthians take over Babylonia.
53 Battle of Carrhae: the Parthians soundly defeat Rome, taking some 10,000 captives.
97 CE The Chinese emissary Gan Ying is sent to visit the Roman Empire. At the Persian Gulf he is persuaded by the Parthians that the rest of the journey is impossibly long and arduous, so returns to China.
224 The Sasanians take over Parthia.

THE BATTLE OF CARRHAE

In the west, the Parthians had to settle a boundary with the expanding Roman Empire, using Armenia as a buffer state between the two. After several military clashes and failed diplomacy, a border was agreed at the Euphrates River.

In 53 BCE Rome broke the agreement when the proconsul of the Syrian province, Marcus Licinius Crassus, a member of the First Triumvirate of Rome, led 44,000 men east into Parthian territory. Rome was burgeoning, and Crassus probably expected an easy victory and personal glory when he faced the Parthians at Carrhae (modern Harran in Turkey). He miscalculated badly. The Parthian horsemen had perfected the art of loosing arrows from horseback, not just while charging forwards, but also while riding away from an enemy, seeming to be in retreat, then turning in the saddle to shoot.

Bust of the Roman proconsul Marcus Licinius Crassus.

GREEK INFLUENCE

Greek influence in Parthian-controlled lands continued for some time. Parthian coins were struck in Greek and the Greek colonies remained important centers of commerce. But apart from Bactria, the Greek centers gradually faded away.

A silver drachma coin of Arsaces I, the founder of the Arsacid Dynasty, includes an inscription of his name in Greek.

Coin of Mithridates I of Parthia. The reverse shows the Greek hero Hercules carrying a lion-skin, a cup and a club.

Coin of the Parthian king Pacorus II.

A fragment from a Parthian monument showing a battle against the Romans.

Parthian captives depicted on the Arch of Septimius Severus in the Roman Forum.

Later known as the "Parthian shot," it is tempting to think that this also gave rise to the saying "a parting shot," but sadly, there is no proof that the Parthians are the origin of the saying.

Some 20,000 Romans, including Crassus, were killed at Carrhae, which effectively stopped the eastward expansion of the Roman Empire and gave the Parthians a lasting reputation as fearsome warriors. About 10,000 Romans were taken captive, and it is thought that some of them later fought as mercenaries in East Asia. It was one of Rome's worst ever defeats.

Carrhae did not produce a lasting peace. Instead, Rome and Parthia remained in a constant state of tension, although there was never again a battle of the same scale.

Rather than outside powers destroying Parthia, in the end it destroyed itself. Civil wars weakened the state so much that in 224 CE the Sasanid dynasty from the Fars province of Iran was able to take over the region.

From 332 BCE Alexander the Great of Macedon conquered the Persian Empire and took over its lands, introducing Greek or Hellenist customs. The process intensified in 176 BCE under Antiochus (IV) Epiphanes of the Seleucid Empire that succeeded Alexander in West Asia. At first the Seleucids had ruled peacefully without trying to impose their beliefs or customs, but Antiochus

THE HASMONEANS

By 166 BCE the Jewish Hasmonean family had had enough of the enforced Hellenization, and launched a revolt against the Seleucids, led by Mattathias and his five sons, including Judah the Maccabee (Hammer). They captured Jerusalem, threw out the Greek idols, and rededicated the Temple. In 142 BCE the Seleucids realized that they had lost control of the region, and withdrew the last of their troops. Judah had won independence.

SALOME ALEXANDRA

Although the Hasmonean or Maccabean kings were liberators, they soon became violent and corrupt, taking the law into their own hands or interpreting laws in their own self-interest. They committed atrocities during their military campaigns and forced conversion on captured people, and in 104–103 BCE Judah Aristobulus killed his mother and a brother to seize power. Civil war broke out against the Hasmonean tyranny, and a religious war began between the Temple priests, the Sadducees, and the Pharisees, the religious party of ordinary people.

Then, in 76 BCE Salome Alexandra, widow of King Alexander Janneus, took the throne. Anxious to build up the country so that it could withstand its powerful neighbors, such as the Roman Empire, she ended the civil war, unifying the people at last. She put a stop to the religious wars by allowing the Pharisees to become part of the religious tribunals, the Sanhedrin, which had previously been run only by the Sadducees, and introduced social reforms such as compulsory primary education for all children, girls as well as boys.

Salome Alexandra strengthened Judah and oversaw a brief Golden Age.

On her death in 67 BCE, however, her unifying influence was lost. Her two sons fought for control of the country, and both appealed to Rome for help. Instead, Rome simply annexed the weakened country. Judah had not enjoyed independence for very long.

Hasmonean Kingdom under Salome Alexandra.

IV appointed pro-Hellenist high priests who brought Greek elements into the Temple, including a statue of the Greek god Zeus.

261 Greeks in Bactria, Afghanistan break away from the Seleucids and declare an independent Hellenistic state, which grows to reach from Turkmenistan to the Punjab.

76–67 Rule of the Hasmonean queen Salome Alexandra in Judea, a Golden Age for the Jews.

ROMAN JUDEA

In 63 BCE the Roman general Pompey crossed from Syria, captured Jerusalem and claimed control of the country, giving it its Roman name of Judea.

Ruling through officials called procurators, Rome faced frequent small-scale revolts. The most serious began in the first century BCE with the development of the Zealot (one who is zealous on behalf of God) movement which opposed foreign rule, then not long later the Roman authorities had to deal with the messianic figure of Jesus Christ, who was crucified around 30 CE.

Aristobulus I.

EAST ASIA: CHINESE TRADITIONS

China is the longest continuous culture in the world, with some features of society dating back to the Shang dynasty (or even earlier). The Shang worshipped their ancestors with sacrifices; Confucius insisted that properly conducted rituals to venerate ancestors could help make a person virtuous in life, and ancestor worship in one form or another continued throughout the centuries even as China experienced huge upheavals.

Today there is less superstition, but the principle of honoring one's dead family members remains as strong as ever, and is still enacted in several festivals and holidays including:

- New Year or the Spring Festival. A time for families to come together and remember their dead.
- The Ghost Festival. A whole month when the gates of the afterlife are supposed to open so that the dead can visit Earth. Families pay respect

CHINESE MEDICINE

Traditional Chinese medicine aimed to strengthen the whole person, rather than just treat the symptoms of a disease, and concentrated on preventing illness and restorating balance to the body. Apart from acupuncture, which today is accepted worldwide as a valid therapy, its major components are:

- diet
- herbal medicine
- moxibustion
- massage
- gentle, therapeutic exercises such as qigong or t'ai chi ch'uan

Another unique and ancient aspect of Chinese culture is its martial arts. Although many originated in later eras, some "internal" martial arts that focus on the qi rather than on brute force, have Daoist origins and can be traced to the Wudang (Wu Tang) mountains in Hubei province, where there were many Daoist monasteries and solitary hermits.

Herbs, tools, and a manual for traditional Chinese medicine.

to their dead ancestors, offering food and drink, or paper money, and also pay respect to lost, wandering ghosts as a sign of compassion (and to prevent being haunted).

- Pure Brightness or Tomb Sweeping Day. A day to honour the ancestors by tidying up tombs.

1000 BCE Kung fu is practiced in China.

162–220 CE Life of General Guan in China. He becomes the popular god of war and martial arts.

200 By now large looms are used in China, enabling large-scale production of cloth.

Early 3rd century The Chinese poet and military leader Cao Cao writes the first commentary on Sun Tzu's *The Art of War*.

Materials for traditional Chinese medicine.

ACUPUNCTURE

Some unique features of Chinese culture date back millennia. By the time of the Han dynasty acupuncture was being used to treat illnesses; its first mention is in a medical encyclopedia compiled from 305 to 204 BCE. Charts were drawn showing the flow of chi (qi or vital energy) around the body, marking the acupuncture points, where tiny needles should be inserted to affect the flow of chi.

A chart showing some of the acupuncture points along meridians of the body.

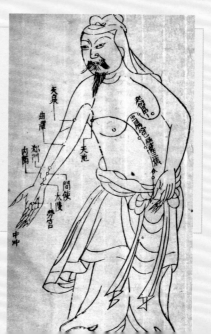

THE FATHER OF MARTIAL ARTS

The "father of martial arts" was not Bruce Lee, but General Guan or Kwan, born in 162 CE. Originally a humble seller of bean-curd, he became such a successful general and adventurer that a Daoist cult sprang up around him, and he became venerated as the god of war and martial arts. Not an aggressor, he was a guard and protector, could control evil spirits and demons, and could prevent war. Public executioners kept their swords in temples dedicated to General Guan, and China's long, massive-bladed halberd was named after him as "General Guan's knife."

The legendary Chinese general Guan.

General Guan's knife.

FORTUNE-TELLING

Ever since the days of the Shang dynasty, fortune-telling was a central part of Chinese culture. The Shang read messages in the cracks in heated tortoise shells, a practice that developed into the divinatory system of the *Yi jing* or *I Ching* (*Book of Change*). This classical Chinese text did not actually offer predictions, but clarified the situation of the questioner and suggested ideas for change.

The questioner throws sticks or coins while asking a question. The pattern of their landing gives rise to either a broken or an unbroken line, and the sequence is repeated until the questioner has a hexagram (six lines). There are 64 of these,

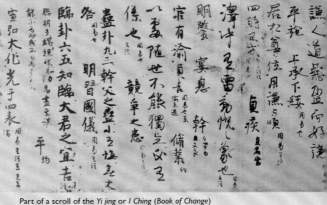

Part of a scroll of the *Yi jing* or *I Ching* (*Book of Change*) written by an emperor in the 9th century CE.

each of which is explained in the *Yi jing* book. Like so many traditional concepts, it centers around an essential harmony in the universe, arguing that the questioner is drawn to creating a particular hexagram at that particular time because everything in the universe is connected.

FENG SHUI

Still popular today, feng shui means "wind and water" and aimed to show the most auspicious sites for villages and houses in terms of the flow of energy. Within a building it indicated the best positioning of furniture and activities.

Chinese feng shui coins for wealth and success.

Apart from during the Qin dynasty, a key feature of ancient Chinese society was the respect given to learning. All government and court officials were scholars as well as administrators, and many emperors would encourage and support their studies. As a result, many important inventions and discoveries were made.

STAR CHARTS

Astronomy was a major study. Festivals and ceremonies were determined by a lunar calendar, so it was vital that correct astronomical records were kept so that calendars were accurate. The court astronomers were respected officials, and were expected to be able to predict eclipses and other heavenly events.

Born around 400 BCE during the Warring States Period, the astronomer Gan De was the first person to observe that Jupiter has moons or satellites. He observed one of the moons with the naked eye, more than 1,000 years before Galileo Galilei "officially" discovered Jupiter's moon with a telescope.

Together with Shi Shen, Gan wrote one of the world's earliest accurate star catalogs, listing more than 100 constellations and thousands of stars. It was far more comprehensive than the first Western star catalog, drawn up by the Greek astronomer Hipparchus in around 129 BCE, which listed some 800 stars.

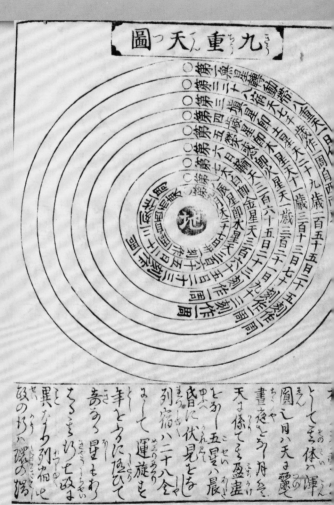

Ancient Chinese astronomy chart shows nine stars or planets circling Earth.

400 BCE Blast furnaces are invented in China to cast iron out of iron ore 1,200 years before it is done in Europe.

364 The Chinese astronomer Gan De makes the first known observation of one of the moons of Jupiter.

c. 83 CE Magnetic compasses are used in China for navigation. Previously fortune-tellers had used lodestones and needles for divination.

c. 105 Cai Lun invents paper in China.

132 Zhang Heng in China builds the first known seismograph to record earthquakes.

142 A Chinese alchemist describes what might be gunpowder.

c. 220 The umbrella is invented in China.

220 Woodblock printing is invented in China, used first on textiles.

220 Classical Chinese landscape painting develops.

577 Primitive matches are invented in China.

THE "EARTHQUAKE WEATHERCOCK"

The world's first seismograph was invented by the scientist Zhang Heng in 132 CE. Named the "earthquake weathercock," it did not predict earthquakes, but recorded when they happened and which direction the shock came from.

His machine is lost, but detailed records of it survive. It was a large bronze jar about 6 feet (1.8 m) in diameter, contained complex mechanisms such as sliding levers, cranks, pivots, and a suspended pendulum. Outside the jar were eight brass dragon heads, each holding a brass ball in its mouth. Around the base of the jar, one beneath each dragon, were eight open-mouthed brass frogs. The whole apparatus was richly decorated.

When an earthquake was felt, the mouth of the dragon in the direction of the shock would open, allowing its ball to fall into the frog's mouth below, and alerting observers that an earthquake had happened, and where the government should send help.

A reconstruction of Zhang Heng's earthquake weathercock.

GUNPOWDER

Gunpowder was probably invented by Daoist alchemists experimenting with different materials in the search for the elixir of life. In 142 CE a man named Wei Boyang described a mixture of three powders that would "fly and dance" violently, which is assumed to be gunpowder (gunpowder is indeed a mixture of three substances). However, the usual date for the discovery of gunpowder is much later, in the 9th century.

The Chinese were the first to use gunpowder.

CAI LUN IS BURIED ALIVE

When Cai Lun invented paper around 105 CE, this remarkable new material was originally met with derision. So Cai Lun devised a melodramatic way of convincing people that paper was, indeed, a magical material: he had himself buried alive in a burning coffin.

Cai Lun arranged with some friends to pretend he was dead, put him in a coffin covered with paper, give him a bamboo tube to breathe through, put the coffin in a grave, and set fire to the paper. He then pushed off the coffin lid and sprang out of the grave.

A Ming-Dynasty woodcut showing steps in traditional papermaking.

Born around 48 CE, Cai Lun was a government official, possibly a eunuch, responsible for delivering messages around the palace and keeping court documents. At that time records were kept on silk, which was extremely expensive, or on thin strips of bamboo, which meant any long piece of writing became ridiculously heavy. Cai Lun was convinced an alternative material could be made, and began experimenting with cloth, bark, and dry grass. He achieved his desired result by pulping bark in water, heating, pounding it, stirring and straining, then drying it in sheets.

This light, thin paper was not very durable, so Cai Lun continued experimenting by adding bits of hemp rope, rags, scraps of silk, or even fishing nets to produce a stronger material.

Despite the initial reaction of ordinary people, the emperor was delighted, and ordered that that paper was to be used throughout the empire. This cheap, durable material was soon eagerly adopted by other Asian countries, too.

PRINTING
The earliest known printed material dates back to 220 CE in China. This was textiles, printed using wood blocks. Adapting the technology for text came later.

THE COMPASS

The Han dynasty also saw the introduction of the compass, made using a naturally magnetic lodestone. Called a "south-governor," it was first used in China for divination and geomancy, and was first used for navigation around 83 CE.

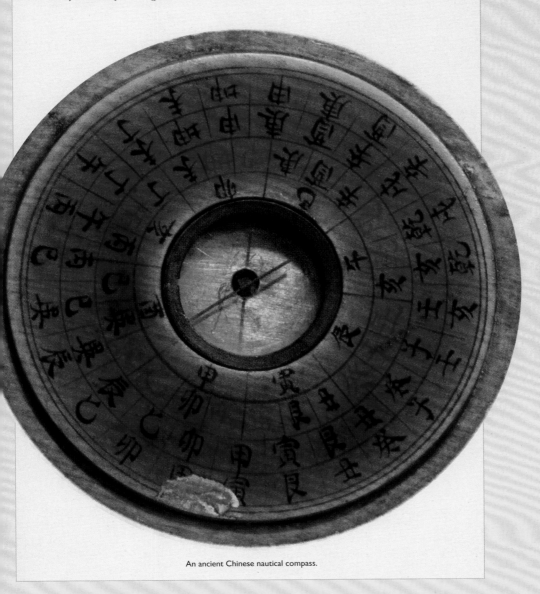

An ancient Chinese nautical compass.

After Seleucid expansion into Greece had been halted at the Battle of Magnesia in 190 BCE, most of Asia Minor had fallen into the hands of Roman allies and client states. Rome itself moved into the eastern Mediterranean during its third period of expansion from 145 BCE. The first Roman territories in Asia were those of the kingdom of Pergamon in Asia Minor, bequeathed to Rome by King Attalus III of Pergamon in 133 BCE. Most of the territory became the Roman province of Asia.

At first the province suffered under Roman rule due to over-exploitation of its vast natural resources and heavy taxation, leading to the people giving their support to the Kingdom of Pontus in its three wars against Rome from 88 to 63 BCE. Named after Mithridates VI, King of Pontus in northern Anatolia from about 120 BCE to 63 BCE, these Mithridatic Wars eventually saw Mithridates forced back through Georgia and then to the Crimea. After this the region recovered and settled into a peaceful and successful province of Rome.

SYRIA

The Roman general Pompey captured Syria, including the Phoenician cities along the Lebanese coast and North Africa, in 64 BCE. The Syrian capital of Antioch became the third largest city in the Roman Empire after Rome itself and Alexandria in Egypt, while the prosperous and bustling province of Syria became one of the most important areas of the empire from the 2nd century CE.

In 106 CE the Nabataean towns in Northern Arabia and Jordan were also annexed by Rome, becoming the province of Arabia Petraea.

Roman ruins in the ancient city of Bosra in Syria. Bosra was the capital of the Roman province of Arabia.

JUDEA

Rome took control of Judah, the area of today's Israel and the Palestinian Territories, from 63 BCE, naming it Judea. At first the Hasmonean kings of Judah were allowed to keep a limited degree of authority, but after a revolt against Rome in 40 BCE, the Empire reclaimed Judea as a full province.

133 BCE Rome inherits the kingdom of Pergamon in Asia Minor and forms the Roman province of Asia.

88–63 The Mithridatic Wars between the Kingdom of Pontus in Asia Minor and Rome.

67 Rome invades Syria.

64 Rome absorbs the final parts of the Seleucid Empire in Syria and Lebanon into the Roman Empire.

63 Rome takes control of Judah, giving it the Roman name of Judea.

53 Battle of Carrhae: the Parthians soundly defeat Rome, taking some 10,000 captives.

50 Brahimi numerals, the foundation of the decimal counting system, are introduced in India.

40 The Hasmonean revolt in Judea against Rome.

ARMENIA AND GEORGIA

The independent kingdom of Armenia was eyed greedily by the Roman, Parthian, and Sasanian Empires, and it was a cause of some of the many Roman–Persian Wars. In 114 CE, the Roman Emperor Trajan conquered it, but was unable to keep control for more than a few years. Finally, in the late 4th century, the Sasanians took control of most of the Armenian kingdom, leaving the rest to Rome. It continued to be a bone of contention until the Muslim Arab armies defeated both empires in the 7th century. Rome exerted an intermittent control over Georgia from the 1st century until the 7th century CE.

HEROD THE GREAT

The son of the Roman administrator of Judea, Herod fled to Rome after the revolt of the last Hasmonean king, Antigonus II. Given an army by the Romans, Herod returned to Judea and eventually defeated Antigonus, executing the rebel. To further his personal dynastic ambitions, he also killed every member of the Hasmonean family that he could find, including his own wife, Mariamne, and his sons by her. Taking the title "the Great," Herod had a great deal of autonomy and became a powerful monarch. An admirer of Greco-Roman culture, he built new cities such as Caesaria, and fortresses such as Masada, as well as extending the kingdom. In Jerusalem he remodeled the Temple into a magnificent building. However, he failed to gain the support and loyalty of the Jews.

When Herod died in 4 BCE his kingdom was divided between his three surviving sons, but neither they nor their sons proved to be able administrators. Rome assumed direct rule in Judea through prefects or procurators.

CARRHAE: A BATTLE TOO FAR

Rome and its successor, the city of Constantinople, carried out regular invasions of lands controlled by the successive Persian empires, and just as regularly had to defend its borders from the Parthians, Seleucids, or Sasanians. There were at least ten different campaigns in what are known as the Roman–Persian Wars.

But Rome's eastward expansion was effectively halted by the Parthian victory at the Battle of Carrhae, southern Turkey, in 53 BCE. The numerically superior Roman invasion force, led by the triumvir Marcus Licinius Crassus, was destroyed by the Parthian archers and cavalry in one of Rome's worst ever military defeats. The horseback archers were particularly effective, firing thousands of arrows that penetrated the Romans' defensive testudo or "tortoise" formation. Although Crassus hoped his army could wait out the storm, and that the Parthians would have to run out of arrows, the Parthians used hundreds of camels to bring replacement arrows to the front. About 20,000 Romans were killed, including Crassus, and 10,000 were captured, with minimal Parthian casualties.

Julius Caesar planned a punitive invasion to extract revenge, but was assassinated before he could carry it out, and when Mark Antony later led a vengeful invasion, he was distracted by civil war as Pompey and Sextus led a revolt. Rome was never to take the Persians' central heartland or venture further into Asia.

The Tusculum portrait, possibly the only surviving sculpture of Julius Caesar made during his lifetime, before his assassination

Mesopotamia and Byzantium

In 116 BCE Rome wrested some territory in Mesopotamia from Parthia, creating a short-lived province. In 198, however, Rome returned and reformed the Mesopotamia province as a buffer between the two empires.

After the fall of the Western Roman Empire in 476, the Eastern Roman Empire or Byzantine Empire took over control of Roman lands, continuing the struggle with Persia.

Crassus, member of Triumvirate with Caesar and Pompeius, wages war against the Parthians but is defeated at Carrhae and executed.

Originally a nomadic Arabian tribe, the Nabataeans moved north and settled in North Arabia, southern Jordan and the Negev, creating a wealthy state. Their capital city of Petra in southwest Jordan was first mentioned in historical records in the early 4th century BCE, but flourished from the 1st century BCE, when the Nabataeans grew rich from the trade caravans that passed through the region.

THE INCENSE ROUTE

Nabataean towns were spread out near the Mediterranean end of the Incense Route from Arabia to the Mediterranean. Luxury goods such as frankincense and myrrh from Arabia, spices, ebony, silk, and precious stones from Southeast Asia, and rare woods and gold from the Horn of Africa were loaded on to camel caravans and taken to the empires of West Asia, Greece, or Rome.

Carved in a canyon out of sandstone cliffs that have veins of red, purple, and

The magnificent ruins of Petra.

yellow running through them, Petra, the "Rose City," was named after the Greek word for "rock." Apart from free-standing buildings such as temples and an amphitheater, the city contained many tombs cut into the cliffs with elaborately carved facades. Overall, there were more than 800 monuments in the city.

Petra had an extensive system of water management, using water channels carved in the rock or ceramic pipes to control flash floods and direct the water into dams and cisterns. This not only provided drinking water but also irrigated the Nabataeans' crops, making Petra an artificial oasis in the desert.

85 BCE–54 CE The Nabataeans, with their capital at Petra in modern Jordan, are at the height of their power.

106 CE Rome conquers the Nabatean towns including Petra.

In 312 BCE the Nabataeans fended off an attack by the Greeks, but they adopted many Greek customs, including some architectural elements. Petra was conquered by Rome in 106 CE, becoming part of the Roman province of Arabia. The city continued to flourish for a while until the trade routes changed, and Palmyra in Syria began to take Petra's place.

The Nabataean city of Shivta in the Negev Desert, Israel.

It takes about 2,000 silkworms to produce 1 pound (c.500 g) of silk, and the process of cultivating the worms, gathering the silk thread, and then spinning it is long and arduous, making the finished product an expensive luxury even before it was carried for thousands of miles to be sold.

Raw silk is spun as one long, continuous filament by the caterpillars or pupae of the blind, flightless silk moth *Bombyx mori*, which is native to China. The worms feed on mulberry leaves (also native to China), then produce a single, long raw silk filament to spin themselves a cocoon inside which they can hatch into the adult moth.

The process is interrupted by the silk cultivator, who gives the silkworm just a few days to enjoy its cocoon, and then kills it with hot air or steam before it can

THE ROADS OPEN

The 4,000-mile-long (6,500 km) trade route across land from China through Persia and on to Europe opened up by accident. In 138 BCE the Chinese general Zhang Qian was sent to the West to find allies in China's long-standing struggle against Xiongnu raiders from the steppes. In Persia he found a trading partner rather than a military partner. China and the Parthian Empire opened formal trading agreements, allowing luxury goods to find their way through Central Asia, through Parthia, and on to the Roman Empire, Europe, Arabia, or North Africa.

Although silk was the most precious commodity that was carried along the Silk Road, pearls from China were also sought after by the Romans, and spices from India were imported too. Traveling in the other direction, fine Roman glassware sometimes made its way to China, along with perfumes and spices from Parthia.

Silkworms growing in their cocoons.

hatch and break the cocoon. A filament can be up to 3,000 feet (950 m) long, and it might take a worm three days to secrete a long enough piece of silk for its cocoon. After the worm is killed, the thread is delicately unwound onto a spool and then twisted with other threads to produce a strand that can be woven with others. When the worm's protective secretion of serocin is washed out, the result is shiny, soft, strong, comfortable, luxurious silk.

138 BCE Chinese General Zhang Qian is sent into the West to find allies against the Xiongnu. His reports on people and routes are said to be the beginning of the Silk Road, the overland trade routes from China to the West.
550 CE Silkworms are smuggled out of China and brought to the Middle East.

Just as importantly, ideas flowed along the trade routes.

There was no one single Silk Road. Instead, routes were chosen depending upon weather, time of year, the presence of bandits, or the presence of soldiers safeguarding parts of the way. Natural hazards varied from desert sandstorms to flash floods, and from mountains to barren plains. Merchants would band

Finished silk threads.

THE SECRET

Archaeological evidence of silk threads, spinning tools, and carvings of silkworms dates back to about 6800 BCE in China. The secret of silk cultivation was carefully preserved for thousands of years. It was a capital crime to take silkworms out of China, and merchants were ordered not to tell foreigners how the material was made.

In an early feat of industrial espionage, one story goes that a Chinese princess hid silkworm eggs in her hair when she went to marry a Central Asian prince in 440. About a hundred years later, two monks visiting China from Byzantium smuggled out silkworm eggs and mulberry seeds inside their walking sticks. A silk industry did eventually grow up in the Middle East, but the high-quality Chinese textiles continued to highly desirable in the West.

A traditional Chinese
silk dress.

A monument in Uzbekistan commemorating travelers along the Silk Roads.

together to travel in large caravans, with plenty of guards.

Goods would often be sold and traded on further along the line several times: few people would have traveled a long distance along the hard, dangerous route.

Middlemen along the Silk Roads, such as the merchants of Sogdia, grew wealthy from trading, taxing, raiding, or protecting caravans. Central Asian towns lucky enough to have good water supplies, such as Merv in Turkmenistan, Samarkand and Tashkent in Uzbekistan, and Bamyan in Afghanistan became rich enough to build grand monuments, places of worship, citadels, and caravanserai, or merchants' inns.

Oddly enough, the Silk Road was safest much later on when nearly the whole length was controlled by the fierce Mongol Empire. The Mongols were keen to benefit from the trade, so kept the roads well-patrolled and free from bandits.

The Silk Road city of Samarkand, Uzbekistan.

Christianity was the second great monotheistic religion to arise in what is today Israel and the Palestinian Territories. It centered round the figure of Jesus Christ, but quickly became more than just a set of religious beliefs. It includes a way of life and a set of cultural ideas.

An altar inside a Christian church.

THE LIFE OF JESUS

Born around 4 BCE in Roman Judea, the historic Jesus was a Jew, the son of a carpenter, Joseph, and his wife Mary. Jesus became a spiritual teacher who was baptized by John the Baptist and began his ministry around 28 CE, preaching a message of love in parables, urging people to repent their sins, performing healings, and debating about how to approach God. He spoke up for sinners and the oppressed.

Jesus's followers believed he was the Messiah, the "anointed one" who was predicted to lead the Jews into salvation and freedom. The title "Christ" is from the Greek for Messiah, which is why he is usually known as Jesus Christ.

Jesus gathered a small but devoted group of followers, in particular the Twelve Disciples or Apostles, and with

c. **4 BCE** Jesus is born in Bethlehem in Roman Judea.

c.**20–33 CE** Ministry of Jesus of Nazareth.

26 Pontius Pilate is appointed Roman procurator of Judea.

c.**30** Jesus Christ is crucified.

c.**45–50** St Paul begins to form the Christian Church and Christianity separates from Judaism.

52 St Thomas, one of Jesus Christ's apostles, arrives in India.

them he went to Jerusalem, where he was welcomed by ordinary people. The Jewish elders, however, challenged his authority and after Jesus shared a last supper with his followers, the elders arranged for him to be arrested. The Jewish tribunal, the Sanhedrin, found him guilty of blasphemy for claiming to be the Messiah, and the Roman authorities crucified him for claiming to be King of the Jews.

The birth of Jesus.

JESUS AND CHRISTIANITY

THE GOSPELS

Jesus's story is found mainly in the four Gospels or revelations of Christ (literally "Good News") found in the New Testament of the Christian holy book, the Bible. Here it is revealed that he was the Son of God, conceived by the Holy Spirit, and his mother was a virgin at the time of his birth. He was sent to earth by God to bring salvation to everyone who believes in him.

On the third day after his death, Jesus rose again and he issued his Great Commission to his disciples: "Go therefore and make disciples of all the nations, baptizing them in the name of the Father and of the Son and of the Holy Spirit ..." He then ascended into Heaven.

Jesus's followers were originally Jews, practicing Judaism and believing that Jesus was the Messiah. It was only when St Paul took the message that Jesus was the Messiah to non-Jews in around 50 CE that a separate religion of Christianity began to develop apart from Judaism.

The crucifixion of Jesus Christ.

ESSENTIAL BELIEFS OF CHRISTIANITY

Christians believe that there is only one God, often called "Father." But they believe in the Trinity, that is God as the Father, God as the Son, and God as the Holy Spirit. Jesus was the Son of God, who was sent to earth to save mankind from sin through his death, as a mark of God's great love for humankind. By believing in Jesus and accepting his sacrifice and resurrection, they can have a relationship with God. Jesus was both fully human and fully God.

Christians believe in life after death, communicate with God through prayer and celebrate the Last Supper through Communion or the Eucharist, where the bread becomes Christ's body and the wine his blood. Some take this metaphorically, others literally, leading to one of the splits within the Christian Church.

Saints are particularly holy people who are formally acknowledged by the Church.

The Christian holy book, the Bible. The word "Bible" derives from the Greek for "books."

THE CHURCH

As Jesus's Disciples, and other converts such as St Paul, spread his message, more non-Jews began to follow the Christian teaching. When an ecclesiastical council decided that they did not have to abide by Jewish Laws, particularly on circumcision, Judaism and Christianity went separate ways.

A formal Church structure developed, with final authority resting with the bishops of Rome, the successors to St Peter, who preached and was martyred for his faith there. The bishops of Rome took the title Pope, meaning "Father." Church councils in the 4th century determined statements of faith and creed, as well as establishing the canon of Holy Scriptures, which includes the Jewish Bible as the Old Testament.

At first persecuted by the Roman emperors, Christianity was accepted by Constantine the Great in 312, then made the official state religion by Theodosius I in 380.

A church in Malacca, Malaysia. Christianity spread to the East with the preachings of Christ's disciple St Thomas.

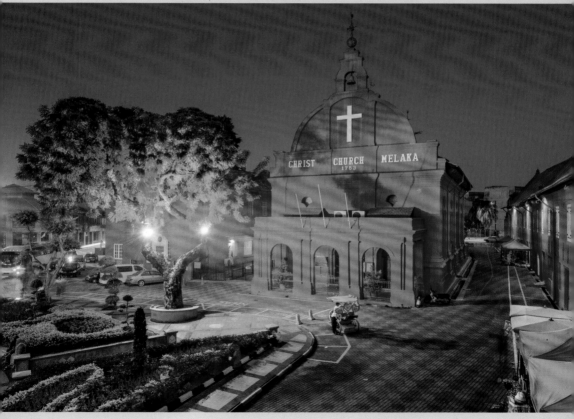

221

The only major revolt against China's long rule in Vietnam was led by a woman, Trung Trac, and her younger sister, Trung Nhi.

Rising up in 40 CE, the Trung Sisters attracted a large army and established an independent state, with Trung Trac declaring herself queen. She ruled for three years until a veteran Chinese general, Ma Yuan, arrived with a large army to re-establish Chinese rule.

Vietnamese and Chinese records have different versions of the story. According to Vietnamese annals, the Trung Sisters grew up learning martial arts and studying military tactics. They saw Vietnamese being treated cruelly by the corrupt Chinese governor, but when Trung Trac's husband stood up to the Chinese, he was killed to deter other protests.

This sparked the rebellion. At first the sisters' army was made up only of women, but they captured 65 states and repelled Chinese attacks for three years. They could not resist Ma Yuan's army however, and when they were abandoned by their

A parade in Saigon in honor of the Trung Sisters.

troops in the midst of losing a battle, they died fighting.

Chinese records deny any mistreatment of Vietnamese people, and say that Ma Yuan beheaded the sisters.

Several myths grew up around these national heroines. One says that they jumped into a river to escape the Chinese army and were turned into statues.

40–43 CE The Trung sisters lead a 3-year rebellion against Chinese rule in Vietnam but are defeated.

Another story holds that the mainly female army ran away in embarrassment when the Chinese soldiers decided to fight naked.

Another celebration in honor of Trung sisters, this time the Hai Ba Trung Temple Festival.

WEST ASIA: THE JEWISH DIASPORA

In 66–70 CE the Jewish Zealots in Judea led a mass rebellion against Rome known as the Great Revolt. It ended in disaster as the Roman emperor Titus destroyed most of Jerusalem and carried off in triumph the treasures of the Temple.

Roman troops umder Emperor Titus destroy the Temple in Jerusalem.

The Arch of Titus in Rome shows Roman soldiers carrying away the treasures of the Jewish Temple.

66–70 Zealot revolt against Rome ends with the destruction of the Temple in Jerusalem. The final Diaspora begins as Jews scatter around the Roman Empire.

73 The last Jewish Zealots kill themselves in the mountain fortress of Masada rather than fall to Rome.

THE BAR KOCHBA REVOLT: DIASPORA

In 132 CE the Jews, led by the soldier Simon bar Kochba, rose up against their Roman rulers. He was defeated and killed in 135 and the revolt had a disastrous ending. Jews were barred from Jerusalem and dispersed throughout the Roman Empire and beyond.

MASADA, THE LAST STAND

The last stand of the Zealots was at the mountain citadel of Masada in the Judean desert from 70 to 73 CE. In this stronghold, the Jewish forces held out for three years, and then the defenders chose to kill themselves rather than submit to Rome.

The mountaintop fortress of Masada, the last stand of the Zealots.

A rdashir I, ruler of the Fars province of Persia from where the first Persian Empire had begun, defeated the Parthians in 224 CE to establish the Sasanian Empire, named after his ancestor Sasan. He took for himself the old title of "King of Kings," and until it collapsed in 651 CE, the Sasanian Empire was a rival to the Eastern and Western Roman Empires.

At their height the Sasanians ruled all of modern Iran, Iraq, the Levant, eastern Arabia, Egypt, and the Caucasus, as well as parts of Turkey, Yemen, Pakistan, and Central Asia.

Although the Sasanians were almost constantly at war with Rome, the Huns, the Turks, and the Byzantines, they encouraged scholarship and the arts. Their

Ardashir I, founder of the Sasanian Empire, captures vassals of the Parthian Empire.

capital city of Ctesiphon was well known for its arts, sciences, and philosophy. Under the reforming king Khosrau I (r. 531–79 CE) the Academy at Gundeshapur was one of the most important centers of learning in the world as it collected manuscripts from neighboring countries.

Weakened by wars, the Sasanians fell to the Arab Caliphate in 651.

224 The Sasanians take over Parthia.
260 The Sasanian king Shapur I captures the Roman emperor, Valerian.
260–262 Odaenathus of Palmyra stops the Sasanian advance in to Syria.

Typical Sasanian art: a silver plate showing the king hunting.

MANICHEISM

Born around 216 CE in Babylonia (now Iraq), the prophet Mani taught a dualistic philosophy in which good and evil battle for supremacy. Good is represented by light and spirit, while evil is represented by darkness and the material world. Although the world is evil and full of pain, Mani taught that the soul shares part of the nature of God, so can be saved and returned to the light through self-knowledge or inner illumination.

Known to his adherents as the "Apostle of Light," Mani thought that his message could replace all other religions. He believed he was just one in a long line of prophets including Buddha, Zarathustra, and Jesus Christ. Prayers, charity, confession, and fasting were important parts of Manichean life.

At first tolerated by the Sasanian emperors, Mani and his followers were later persecuted, as they were in the Roman Empire. However his message spread to India and China in the east. Mani supposedly wrote several books, but they were lost from the Middle Ages onward until portions were discovered in the 20th century. He died in Persia between 274 and 277.

According to one story, Mani was beheaded and his head and body were displayed at the gates of the city of Gundeshapur.

Fond of large buildings, the Sasanians adapted art forms from other countries to create their own styles. The city of Ardashir-Khwarrah (formerly Gur and now Firuzabad), was constructed by Ardashir I with a circular plan, whereas his son Shapur I used a grid design for his city of Bishapur. The palaces in these cities and at Ctesiphon shared some characteristics such as iwans, halls with open vaulting on at least one side, but also had different features such as various arrangements of domes and cupolas. Sasanian buildings were decorated with stucco and other ornamentation, and often had mosaic pavements.

The Sasanians were also skilled metalworkers, and in particular crafted silver or gold "shell" bowls, with the inner surface of the shell etched into a relief scene, usually of a king hunting on horseback. But the most distinctive feature of Sasanian art was huge rock carvings depicting coronation or triumphal scenes. Although they were found all over the kingdom, many of the carvings were made near the Achaemenid tombs at Persepolis or Naqsh-e Rustam, as if the Sasanians were establishing a link to the glorious past.

Few Sasanian statues survive, but the Colossal Statue of Shapur I, placed in a cave near Bishapur, shows the skill of the stoneworkers. About 22 feet (6.7 m) tall, the statue measures 6.5 feet (2 m) across the shoulders.

Sasanian art had a major influence on Islamic culture, but also on artistic developments much further afield, in China, India, Africa, and Western Europe.

CHINESE ENVOYS

In 97 CE a Chinese diplomatic mission set off on the long journey into the west to visit Rome. Led by Gan Ying, the party reached the Persian Gulf safely, only to be convinced by the Parthians there that the next stage of the journey would have to be a long, difficult and dangerous sea voyage around the Arabian peninsula.

Disheartened, the Chinese returned home, not realizing that they had been duped. The Parthians were desperate to keep their control of the Silk Roads, and feared that if China and Rome made direct contact they might establish a maritime trade route or some other way around the Parthian lands. We do not know how the would-be diplomats explained their failure to the Chinese emperor, or what he said to them in return.

In order to establish direct trade relations with Rome, Gan Ying was dispatched by Ban Chao to the Roman empire in 97 CE.

By 1000 BCE the city of Palmyra in modern Syria was well known to other states in West Asia. Sitting on an oasis in the desert 134 miles (215 km) northeast of Damascus, Palmyra also had several springs which made agriculture possible. Inhabited by an ethnic mixture of Arabs, Amorites, Arameans, and Jews, the city eventually grew wealthy from trade, sending caravans along the Silk Road and through the Roman Empire.

The Temple of Bel in Palmyra.

Palmyrenes spoke a dialect of Aramaic while using Greek for commerce, and their art and architecture reflected a mixture of eastern and western influences. Their wealth enabled the construction of great buildings such as the Temple of Bel

c.2000 BCE The first historical mention of Palmyra (in modern Syria) is as a trade contract with an Assyrian colony.

180 By now the first tower tombs and city temples are built in Palmyra, Syria.

260–2 CE Odaenathus of Palmyra stops the Sasanian advance in to Syria.

267 Queen Zenobia of Palmyra builds the Palmyrene Empire and later rebels against Rome.

and the Great Colonnade. This "main street" stretched for more than half a mile (1.1 km) through the city and was adorned with features such as a monumental arch and bronze statues of prominent citizens.

Built outside the city walls was a necropolis of mainly tower-shaped tombs, most containing funerary busts.

Palmyra was ruled by various empires such as the Assyrians and Seleucids, and at its height in the 3rd century CE it was an autonomous subject of the Roman Empire. Roman-period buildings included baths and an amphitheater, and the population may have been as high as 200,000.

The Palmyrene King Odaenathus.

THE PALMYRENE EMPIRE

In the mid 3rd century CE the rise of the Sasanian Persian empire threatened Palmyra's trade routes. Rome was weakened by internal conflict at the time, so the Palmyrene lord Odaenathus was appointed by the city to defend its interests. He first tried diplomacy, which was rejected, so he turned to war. In 260 he won a decisive battle against the Persians near the Euphrates river, then went on to push the Persians out of Roman Mesopotamia and quell Roman rebels in the region.

Odaenathus declared himself king, and when he died in 267 CE his widow Zenobia expanded the kingdom into an empire, claiming control of Egypt among other areas. Zenobia directed her troops herself from horseback, and although she tried at first not to antagonize Rome – even issuing coins featuring the Roman Emperor Aurelian – when she declared independence then took the title of empress in 271, Rome reacted badly.

Aurelian's armies advanced into Syria and Egypt on a punitive expedition, retaking control and defeating Zenobia in several battles. She was captured and taken to Rome, and in 273 Aurelian destroyed Palmyra, taking many of its statues back to Rome. Zenobia was not executed, and she later married a Roman senator.

Although Emperor Diocletian later restored the city, it lost prominence and declined into nothing more than a village. Its ancient buildings remained, however, until partly flattened by Islamic extremists in the 21st century.

The Great Colonnade in Palmyra.

Zenobia in chains in Rome. She went on to marry a Roman senator.

After the Bar Kochba Revolt in 132–35 CE, Jewish people were left without a Temple and the center of their religious identity. However, the religious center of Judaism then moved to the academy at Yavneh, whose rabbinical council formed the new Sanhedrin, the Jewish legislative and judicial body.

Synagogues became the focus of Jewish communities, and the Sadducee sect, which was tied to Temple rituals and sacrifices, died out. Rabbis, the scholars or teachers, replaced priests.

The Yavneh rabbis were determined to make sure that oral teachings which explained and expounded upon the Torah would not be lost. So, they were collected together as the Mishna, or Oral Law, a process that was completed by around 210. This also enabled the Jewish communities who were scattered around

A rabbi reading from the Torah in a synagogue. Synagogues became the focus of Jewish communities after the destruction of the Temple.

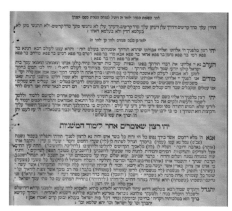

A page from the Mishna, the collection of Jewish oral law teachings.

132–135 CE The Bar Kochba Revolt against Rome in Judea ends in disaster for the Jews. They are barred from Jerusalem and the final Jewish Diaspora continues.

the Roman Empire to all keep the same, standard traditions.

Although some exiles did return to rebuild communities in Roman Palestine, the region remained a quiet backwater, even when taken over by the Muslim Caliphate in the 7th century.

A student before two rabbis.

235

After the decline of the Mauryan Empire in 185 BCE, the two largest kingdoms in India were the Satavahanas, who ruled the Deccan, and the Kushans, who created a large territory in the north, extending through Afghanistan, Bactria, and to northwest China. Originally a branch of the Yuezhi confederation of nomads from the steppes, in the 3rd century CE the Kushans in Afghanistan were subjugated by the Persian Sasanids, and the following century they were supplanted by the Guptas in north India.

It is not clear where the Gupta kings came from, but in 320 Chandra Gupta began to form an empire. He made a dynastic marriage to the princess

The shaded area shows the extent of the Gupta empire under Chandra Gupta III.

Kumaradevi who belonged to a large clan ruling Magadha, modern day Bihar, and by 321 he had conquered or assimilated that kingdom along with other states from the Ganges to Allahabad in Uttar Pradesh. He took the title "King of Kings."

THE HORSE SACRIFICE

Chandra's son Samudra Gupta succeeded him in 335, reigning until 380 and conquering more than 20 kingdoms. He extended his control over the entire north and central India, as well as Sri Lanka, Kashmir, and Afghanistan. Pataliputra in present day Patna became his capital.

Samudra commemorated his territorial conquests with a Vedic ritual horse sacrifice known as Ashwamedha. A stallion, followed by 100 young warriors, would be released on the borders of the kingdom to wander for a year. Wherever the horse roamed the local chief could challenge the imperial authority and battle the warriors. If the chief did not fight, it meant he acknowledged the king's sovereignty.

At the end of the year, if the horse had not been captured or killed, it would be brought back to the king's capital where it would be ritually sacrificed, along with hundreds of other animals. The horse was a symbol of the sun, so the horse sacrifice represented the annual renewal of the sun at the New Year, and the renewal of the king's rule.

c.320 CE The Gupta dynasty begins to control northern and central India. Temples are built and and large sculptures of gods created.

399 The Chinese Buddhist monk Faxian sets out to visit India. His record of his travels is an important historical document.

4th century The Indian epic poem the *Mahabarata* is finalized.

Special coins were minted to celebrate Samudra's horse sacrifice ritual.

Samudra is said to have loved poetry, and other coins depict him playing the lyre. A record of Samudra Gupta's exploits was inscribed on the Ashokan Pillar in Allahabad, one of the pillars that the Mauryan emperor Ashoka had first inscribed in the 3rd century BCE.

"SUN OF VALOR"

Chandra Gupta II, Samudra's successor, reigned from 350 to 415. He gained even more territories through marriages and conquests, giving the empire its greatest extent. With an enormous military force, Chandra Gupta II was known as "Sun of Valor." His standing army included 500,000 infantry, 50,000 cavalry, 20,000 charioteers, and 10,000 elephants. His navy consisted of 1,200 ships.

Despite his military prowess, his reign is particularly known for its intellectual and cultural achievements, recorded by the Chinese traveling monk Faxian.

GUPTA CULTURAL ACHIEVEMENTS

Final editing of the *Ramayana* and the *Mahabharata* took place in the Gupta period, probably under Chandra Gupta II. The manual of sexual behavior, the *Karma Sutra*, may have been compiled in this period, the mathematician Aryabahata was working, and great paintings were created.

The poet and playwright Kalidasa, held by some to be the greatest poet and dramatist in the Sanskrit language, may have worked at the court of Chandra

FAXIAN

Born in 337 in Shanxi, Faxian was a Buddhist monk and translator who walked all the way from China to India to collect Buddhist texts. Setting out in 399 with nine others, he reached India from the northwest during the reign of Chandra Gupta II. Faxian wrote a detailed journal of his observations as he traveled to Buddhist shrines, collecting sacred works and images.

Faxian praised the Gupta administration for being well organized and liberal. Highways were safe, taxes low, and government officials were well paid so were honest and fair. He reported that people were prosperous and happy, rest-houses and hospitals were available for the poor and needy, and that Hindus, Jains, and Buddhists lived together peacefully.

Faxian left India by sea in 411, returning to China where he translated his Buddhist texts. He died in 422.

Faxian, a Chinese Buddhist monk who traveled by foot from China to India, returns to China after fifteen years.

A coin of Chandragupta II.

Gupta II, who patronized nine great scholars known as "jewels."

The Guptas saw the first period of elaborate temple-building using dressed stone and brick. The iconic, carved stone deity statue also emerged during the Guptas' period and the angular style of sculpture developed into flowing, gently curved lines.

Kumara Gupta (reigned c.415–55) founded the Nalanda University in Magadha. Scholars came from as far afield as Tibet, China, Korea, and Central Asia, and the university also had links with the Shallendra dynasty of Indonesia. Subjects studied included the Vedas, logic, Sanskrit, medicine, and the texts of Buddhism. Mahayana Buddhism was developed there, but despite all the artistic achievements, the caste system had developed and the status of women deteriorated.

After internal conflicts and external pressures, the Empire shrank and faded in the 6th century.

Ruins of Nalanda University, Bihar, India.

orn in India in 476 CE, the mathematician Aryabhata was only 23 when he wrote his important mathematical book, the *Aryabhatiya*. This summarized the state of knowledge of Indian math, and also presented his own work.

Although he presumably did not invent the concepts, Aryabhata wrote about place-values and the use of zero as a number in its own right. The idea of zero to express the lack of a value in a large number had been familiar to Babylonian mathematicians, for example 4050, where there are no single units and there is no value in the hundreds. But it was Indian mathematicians who realized that since some mathematical expressions produce the number zero, it should be treated just like any other number. This led to the use in math of numbers that are less than zero, that is negative numbers.

595 CE The Hindu–Arabic number system is established, the basis of the system used today **before 600** Chess is invented in India.

The *Aryabhatiya* influenced later Arab scholars and was one of the works that introduced zero and place-values to the Middle East and from there eventually to Europe, giving rise to the Hindu-Arabic numbers we use today.

The evolution of Hindu-Arabic numerals from the 1st century to the 16th century.

Aryabhata.

From the far west of the Eurasian plains to the far east, the nomadic steppe dwellers were all described by their more settled neighbors as living in yurts on carts.

c.**600** BCE A bronze bowl in the Zagros Mountains of Iran is decorated with the earliest known picture of a yurt.

TYPES OF CART YURTS

There were two types of "yurts on carts." First there were the ones that were disassembled and packed away when the nomads moved. The second type was mounted permanently on a cart, and while the man might ride a horse, his family would remain inside their hut as they moved.

YURTS

Known as gers in Mongolia, yurts are still used today. Simple round tents with felt or hide coverings around a collapsible wooden frame, they are light to carry, can be packed up and reassembled quickly, and protect against the sometimes freezing winds on the steppes. It is thought that their design has hardly changed for thousands of years in Central Asia.

Groups in Siberia claim their ancestors first used yurts, and the tents were shown on a bronze bowl found in the Zagros Mountains, dating to about 600 BCE. Chinese writers reported that members of the nomadic Xiongnu confederacy (209 BCE–93 CE) carried felt-covered tents on their carts, and Greek commentators also described the mobile homes of the nomads they met.

Genghis Khan sometimes ruled his medieval Mongolian Empire from a large ger fixed on a huge cart pulled by 22 oxen. However, the ones used by Central Asians in the east were small, family-sized rather than emperor-sized, and rather than being a tent on a cart, were simply carts with a basic framework covered by felt.

In his *Prometheus Bound*, the Greek tragedian Aeschylus described homes of the Scythians as "... basketwork huts, high up on wheels, like wagons."

And in 378 CE the Roman General Ammianus Marcellinus reported on the nomads known as the Alans: "... they have no huts ... and dwell in wagons, which they cover with rounded canopies of bark and drive over the boundless wastes."

As for the Huns, Marcellinus wrote: "They are all without fixed abode, without hearth, or law, or settled mode of life, and keep roaming from place to place, like fugitives, accompanied by the wagons in which they live; in wagons their wives weave for them their hideous garments, in wagons they cohabit with their husbands, bear children ..."

It is difficult to tell what he found most disgusting – their clothes, or the fact that they were simply living a nomadic lifestyle, as the steppe peoples have done for millennia.

Reconstruction of the rolling home of Genghis Khan, Ulaan Baatar, Mongolia.

After the decline of the Han dynasty in China, it would be several hundred years before the country enjoyed a matching period of dynamism and strength.

First, three kingdoms fought for supremacy, then the Western Jin dynasty that eventually emerged supreme was overrun by nomads from the north and abandoned control over the Yellow River valley. Under the Eastern Jin, the capital moved to what is now Nanjing. The country split again into Northern and Southern Dynasties, before finally the Sui took a grip on the seat of power in 581.

The Sui made a good start. They opened examination centers for the civil service all round the country, instead of just at the capital, allowing more candidates to apply to be government officials. This had the effect of raising standards overall. The Sui

A Sui-Dynasty Buddhist bodhisattva statue.

A Sui-Dynasty "wu zhu" coin. Named after their weight (one zhu weighed 100 millet seeds and the coin weighed five zhus), wu zhus were minted for hundreds of years.

also reformed the legal code, and built the Great Canal, linking the Yellow and the Yangtze rivers. They then made a costly mistake, launching other expensive and ambitious projects that needed conscripted labor. By 605 the spirit of rebellion was in the air again.

China ended this early period of its history with another major change underway. For a long time no one had been able to offer strong leadership and defend the borders, and as a result northern China had been suffering from the curse of bandit raids. By 400 CE people were drifting away from this danger zone to the lower Yangtze valley, even though it was full of swamps and jungles that had to be cleared and drained through canals, reservoirs, and dams. Slowly, the Yangtze valley's agricultural output began to outstrip that of the North China Plain.

200 China attempts to crush the Mongolian Xiongnu but is defeated. The two states divide their territory at the Great Wall.

164 According to tradition, Prince Liu An from northern China creates tofu, or bean curd, by pressing coagulated soy milk into chunks.

150 The Xiongnu cross the Great Wall and take control of China north of the Yellow River.

138 Chinese General Zhang Qian is sent into the West to find allies against the Xiongnu. His reports on people and routes are said to be the beginning of the Silk Roads, the overland trade routes from China to the West.

128 An overland trade route between China and India is forged across northern Burma.

121 China repels the Xiongnu and pushes them north of the Gobi desert.

111 China conquers a large part of Vietnam.

108 China founds colonies in Manchuria and northern Korea.

100 In the Bronze Age the Malay Peninsula becomes a maritime trading crossroads for goods from India, Egypt, the Middle East, Java and China.

91 Sima Qian, the "father of Chinese historians," completes his literary history of China.

c.60 Having been displaced by the Mongolian Xiongnu, a group of nomadic Yuezhi people begin to form the Kushan Empire centered in Afghanistan. The Kushans will help develop the Silk Roads and allow Buddhism to be transmitted to China.

9–23 CE The Xin (New) dynasty in China rebels against the Han and ends abuses by landowners and nobles.

25 CE The New Eastern Han dynasty overthrows the Xin in China.

57 A Chinese record is the first written mention of Japan.

68 Buddhist monks from India arrive in China.

80 Burial of the "Jade Princess," Princess Douwan, in China. Her burial suit is made of 2,160 pieces of jade sewn together by gold wire.

A Terracotta Army carriage with an umbrella securely fixed to the side.

c.83 Magnetic compasses are used in China for nagivation. Previously fortune-tellers had used lodestones and needles for divination.

90 A Chinese army attacking the Kushans reaches the Caspian Sea, the furthest west China reached.

97 The Chinese emissary Gan Ying is sent to visit the Roman Empire. At the Persian Gulf he is persuaded by the Parthians that the rest of the journey is impossibly long and arduous, so returns to China.

c.100 The chain pump, allowing for better irrigation (and better crops) is used in China. Ship's rudders and suspension bridges are also used in China.

c.105 Cai Lun invents paper in China.

132 Zhang Heng in China builds the first known seismograph to record earthquakes.

166 A group of Roman merchants or diplomats arrive in China, having traveled via Vietnam.

c.167 Himiko, an elderly priestess, unites several small Japanese states into one.

184–205 Yellow Turbans Revolt against the Han in China.

c.200 Buddhism is introduced to Tibet.

c.200 People in Mindinao, the Philippines, create unique anthropomorphic burial jars, the Maitum Jars, each with individual facial features, possibly those of the person whose remains are in the jar.

Trays of hand-carved Chinese wooden movable type characters for printing,

A sculpture from a Chinese tea house.

200 By now, large looms are used in China, enabling large-scale production of cloth.

Early 3rd century The Chinese poet and military leader Cao Cao writes the first commentary of Sun Tzu's *The Art of War*.

220 China descends into the civil wars of the Three Kingdoms.

220 Woodblock printing is invented in China, used first on textiles.

220 Classical Chinese landscape painting develops.

c.220 The umbrella is invented in China.

250 Tea becomes a popular drink in China

300 Metal stirrups are used for horse-riding in China.

316 Having been allowed to settle in northern China, nomads and semi-nomads from the steppes take over Luoyang. The Jin abandon the Yellow River valley and move to what is now Nanjing, beginning the Eastern Jin period.

372 Buddhism is introduced to Korea.

c.380 Pure Lands Buddhism develops in China.

399 The Chinese Buddhist monk Faxian sets out to visit India. His record of his travels is an important historical document.

c.400–500 Raiders force northern Chinese people to move into the lower Yangtze valley. There the land is cleared and drained and becomes more productive than the North China Plain.

c.450 The largest grave in the world, the Daisen Kofun burial mound, is built in Japan for Emperor Nintoku.

c.495 The Shaolin Temple, home of Chinese martial arts, is built in Henan Province, about 20 miles (30 km) from Luoyang.

c.526 The Indian Buddhist Bodhidharma arrives in China. He founds Zen or Chan Buddhism.

538 or 552 Buddhism is introduced to Japan.

550 Silkworms are smuggled out of China and brought to the Middle East.

577 Primitive matches are invented in China.

581 The Sui dynasty begin legal and administrative reforms in China.

c.581 Blocks of pressed tea are first used as currency in China. Tea is now drunk for its pleasant taste, not just for medicinal reasons.

588 The Sui dynasty reunites China.

c.600 The name "Shinto," meaning "way of the gods," is adopted in Japan for the indigenous religious cult.

605 China's Grand Canal opens, linking the Yellow and the Yangtze rivers.

607 The Horyu-ji Buddhist temple is built in Nara, Japan. Its pagoda is the oldest surviving wooden building in the world.

Sima Qian (father of Chinese historians)

KAABA

Built of granite and marble and usually covered by a ceremonial black cloth called the kiswah, the Kaaba is in the center of the Great Mosque in Mecca, Saudi Arabia. It is the holiest site in all Islam and all Muslims, wherever they are in the world, face towards the Kaaba when they pray. The Muslims' holy book, the Koran, decrees that all Muslims who are able to do so should visit the Kaaba on a pilgrimage called the hajj at least once in their lifetimes. Part of this involves walking seven times around the Kaaba in an anti-clockwise direction, which is called making the tawaf. The most significant time to make the pilgrimage is during the annual ceremonial hajj period, when millions of Muslims arrive in Mecca.

Islamic pilgrims circumambulating the holiest site in Islam, the Kaaba in Mecca, Saudi Arabia.

Born around 570 CE in Mecca, Arabia (now in Saudi Arabia), Muhammad was orphaned when he was very young, and was put in the care of first his grandfather and then his uncle. He belonged to the impoverished but respectable Banu Hashim family of the Quraysh tribe.

As a young teenager, Muhammad worked for his uncle in a camel caravan, traveling to Syria and later to the Indian Ocean. He gained a reputation for honesty, indicated by his nickname "al-Amin," meaning "trustworthy" or "faithful."

In his early twenties, Muhammad began working for Khadihah, a wealthy merchant woman fifteen years older than him, and the two got married.

A deeply devout man, Muhammad would often go to pray and meditate in a cave near Mecca. In 610, while meditating there, he received the first revelation from the Angel Gabriel. Although the Islamic calendar did not start for a few more years, this first revelation heralded the beginning of the end of the ancient world in Asia.

570 Birth of Muhammad
610 Muhammad receives his first revelation, heralding the beginning of the Muslim era and the end of the ancient world.

As directed by the Angel, Muhammad remembered and recited these revelations, which formed the text of the Koran. His wife and cousin were the first to believe he was a prophet, and to accept his basic message that there is only one God. His name is Allah, and Muhammad was his messenger. But when he began to preach publicly and oppose idol worship and polytheism, Muhammad offended the local rulers.

In 622 Muhammad and his followers felt they had to flee Mecca for Medina. This journey, known as the Hegira (migration), marked the year that the Islamic calendar began. The religion that Muhammad preached was known as Islam (Submission), and Muslim means "one who submits" [to God].

A fifteenth-century Indian Koran.

MUSEUMS

American Museum of Natural History, New York, USA
Antiquities Museum, Caesarea, Israel
Ashmolean Museum, Oxford, UK
Asian Art Museum of San Francisco, USA
Azerbaijan Museum, Tabriz, Iran
Babylonian Collection, Yale University, USA
Bible Lands Museum, Jerusalem, Israel
British Museum, London, UK
Cincinnati Art Museum, Cincinnati, USA
Field Museum, Chicago, USA
Five Continents Museum, Munich, Germany
Hatay Archaeology Museum, Antakya, Turkey
Honolulu Museum of Art, Honolulu, USA
Hood Museum of Art, Dartmouth College, Hanover, New Hampshire, USA
Indian Museum, Kolkata, India
Iraq Museum, Baghdad, Iraq
Israel Bible Museum, Safed, Israel
Israel Museum, Jerusalem, Israel
Istanbul Archaeology Museum, Istanbul, Turkey
Metropolitan Museum of Art, New York, USA
Miho Museum, Koka, Japan
Montreal Museum of Fine Art, Montreal, Canada
Musée Cernuschi, Paris, France
Musée du Louvre, Paris, France
Musée du quai Branly, Paris, France
Musée Guimet, Paris, France
Museo Arqueológico Nacional, Madrid, Spain
Museo Nacional de Arte Oriental, Buenos Aires, Argentina
Museu Nacional de Arqueologia, Lisbon, Portugal
Museum of Anatolian Civilizations, Ankara, Turkey
Museum of Asian Art, Berlin, Germany
Museum of Asian Art, University of Malaya, Malaysia
Museum of Fine Arts, Boston, USA
Museum of Oriental Art, Torino, Italy

National Museum, Beijing, China
National Museum, Jakarta, Indonesia
National Museum, New Delhi, India
National Museum of Anthropology, Luzon, Philippines
National Museum of China, Beijing, China
National Museum of Colombo, Colombo, Sri Lanka
National Museum of Beirut, Beirut, Lebanon
National Museum of Iran, Tehran, Iran.
National Museum of Iraq, Baghdad, Iraq
National Museum of Korea, Seoul, South Korea
National Museum of Oriental Art, Rome, Italy
National Museum of Japanese History, Sakura, Japan
National Palace Museum, Taipei, Taiwan
Oriental Institute Museum – University of Chicago
Palace Museum, Beijing, China
Pergamon Museum, Berlin, Germany
Pierpont Morgan Library, New York, USA
Potala Palace, Lhasa, Tibet
Sanxingdui Museum, Guanghan, China
Seattle Art Museum, Seattle, USA
Semitic Museum, Harvard University, USA
Shaanxi History Museum, Xi'an, China
Shanghai Museum, Shanghai, China
Smithsonian Institution, Washington, USA
Terracotta Army Museum, Xi'an, China
Tokyo National Museum, Tokyo, Japan
University of Cambridge Museum of Archaeology and Anthropology, Cambridge, UK
University of Chicago Oriental Institute, Chicago, USA
University of Pennsylvania Museum of Archaeology and Anthropology, Philadelphia, USA
Vatican Museum, Vatican City, Rome
Victoria and Albert Museum, London, England

BIBLIOGRAPHY

Bahrani, Z. *Mesopotamia: Ancient Art and Architecture.*

Bauer, Susan Wise. *The Story of the World: History for the Classical Child,* Vol. 1.

Bingham, Jane. *The Usborne Internet-linked Encyclopedia of the Ancient World.*

Cline, Eric H. *1177 BC.*

Cotterell, Arthur. *Asia: A Concise History.*

Dalal, Roshen. *The Compact Timeline History of the World.*

Ebrey, Patricia Buckley. *The Cambridge Illustrated History of China.*

Editors, Charles River. *The Empires of Ancient Persia: The History and Legacy of the Achaemenids, Parthians, and Sassanids in Antiquity*

Editors, Charles River. *Sumer: The History of the Cities and Culture that Established Ancient Mesopotamia's First Civilization.*

Frankfort, Henri. *The Art and Architecture of the Ancient Orient.*

Haywood, John. *The Penguin Historical Atlas of Ancient Civilisations.*

Holcombe, Charles. *A History of East Asia.*

Huang, Ray. *China—A Macro History.*

Lassieur, Allison. *Ancient Mesopotamia (Ancient World)*

Leick, Gwendolyn. *Mesopotamia: The Invention of the City.*

Liu, Jing. *Foundations of Chinese Civilization: The Yellow Emperor to the Han Dynasty (2697 BCE–220 CE).*

Liu, Xinru. *Ancient India and Ancient China: Trade and Religious Exchanges, AD 1–600.*

Loveday, Helen et al. *Iran: Persia Ancient and Modern.*

MacArdle, Meredith. *The Timeline History of China.*

Marr, Andrew. *A History of the World.*

Marriott, Emma. *The History of the World in Bite-Sized Chunks.*

Martell, Hazel Mary. *The Kingfisher Book of the Ancient World.*

Parker, Edward Harper. *Ancient China Simplified.*

Roberts, J.M. *The New Penguin History of the World.*

Scott, Michael. *Ancient Worlds: An Epic History of East and West.*

Van De Mieroop, Marc. *A History of the Ancient Near East, ca. 3000–323 BC (Blackwell History of the Ancient World).*

Woolf, Alex. *The Ancient World: 4500–500 BCE.*

A to Z of the Ancient World.

The Timechart History of Jewish Civilization.

WEBSITES

Ancientchina.co.uk

Ancientindia.co.uk

Mesopotamia.co.uk

INDEX

INDEX